AF324877

WOMEN ENTREPRENEURS IN NORTH AFRICA

Historical Frameworks, Ecosystems and New Perspectives for the Region

WOMEN ENTREPRENEURS IN NORTH AFRICA

Historical Frameworks, Ecosystems and New Perspectives for the Region

Editors

Léo-Paul Dana
Dalhousie University, Canada

Dina Modestus Nziku
University of the West of Scotland, UK

Ramo Palalić
Sultan Qaboos University, Oman

Veland Ramadani
South-East European University, North Macedonia

World Scientific

NEW JERSEY · LONDON · SINGAPORE · BEIJING · SHANGHAI · HONG KONG · TAIPEI · CHENNAI · TOKYO

Published by

World Scientific Publishing Co. Pte. Ltd.

5 Toh Tuck Link, Singapore 596224

USA office: 27 Warren Street, Suite 401-402, Hackensack, NJ 07601

UK office: 57 Shelton Street, Covent Garden, London WC2H 9HE

British Library Cataloguing-in-Publication Data
A catalogue record for this book is available from the British Library.

WOMEN ENTREPRENEURS IN NORTH AFRICA
Historical Frameworks, Ecosystems and New Perspectives for the Region

Copyright © 2022 by World Scientific Publishing Co. Pte. Ltd.

All rights reserved. This book, or parts thereof, may not be reproduced in any form or by any means, electronic or mechanical, including photocopying, recording or any information storage and retrieval system now known or to be invented, without written permission from the publisher.

For photocopying of material in this volume, please pay a copying fee through the Copyright Clearance Center, Inc., 222 Rosewood Drive, Danvers, MA 01923, USA. In this case permission to photocopy is not required from the publisher.

ISBN 978-981-123-660-0 (hardcover)
ISBN 978-981-123-661-7 (ebook for institutions)
ISBN 978-981-123-662-4 (ebook for individuals)

For any available supplementary material, please visit
https://www.worldscientific.com/worldscibooks/10.1142/12266#t=suppl

Desk Editor: Nicole Ong

Typeset by Diacritech Technologies Pvt. Ltd.
Chennai - 600106, India

Dedicated to Loulou Akerib (1890–1968), entrepreneur who arrived in North Africa from Western Asia by camel caravan in 1894. She neither married nor had children of her own but mothered many with unselfish love.

© 2022 World Scientific Publishing Company
https://doi.org/10.1142/9789811236600_fmatter

Contents

© 2022 World Scientific Publishing Company
https://doi.org/10.1142/9789811236600_fmatter

Foreword by Professor David A Kirby

Holder of The Queen's Award for Enterprise Promotion.
Former Vice President, The British University in Egypt

Every year when I start a new entrepreneurship course, I ask the class to name me an entrepreneur. The first thing we learn is that entrepreneurs are male. Of course that is not true, but the list I am given almost always comprises male names only. Indeed, Candida Brush (1997: 14) once observed that *"so often the first image one has of an entrepreneur is a man"* while the Canadian management guru, Henry Mintzberg (1973: 128), made the point that *not only is "the entrepreneur to be found at the helm of a small business, where innovation is the key to survival" [but] "**He** may also be found at the head of, or within, a large organisation that is changing rapidly."*

The reason why we think of entrepreneurs as men is that, traditionally, there have been significantly more men running their own businesses than women. The first ever extra-curricular entrepreneurship programme I ran was for women in Wales in the early 1980s. We observed that women were significantly under-represented in the workforce in this part of the UK and so, as there were few jobs, we trained them in how to start and manage a small business, at the same time introducing them to the then new computer technology. While start-up programmes were not common at that time, this was the first programme specifically focussed on women.

Since then things have changed but as the GEM Women's Entrepreneurship Report for 2018/19 demonstrates, there are only 9 countries globally where women report entrepreneurial behaviours equal to (on parity with) or greater than those of men. In the MENA Region (Middle East and North Africa), the subject of much of this book, women account for only 9% of the Total Entrepreneurial Activity (TEA) of the region, second lowest only to Europe.

In the 10 years that I lived and worked in the region, I could never discover why this was the case. It is not to do with religion as the prophet Mohamed's first wife, Khadija, "Mother of the Believers," was a successful business woman in her own right. Also, countries in the Region with the same religion show different rates. Neither is it to do with the lack of role models as Syeed and Zafar (2014) demonstrate in "Arab Women Rising." There are many highly effective female entrepreneurs in the region who demonstrate what women can achieve and contribute. However, early research by Hattab (2012) on the topic and the region points to the lack of literature and reliable statistics "discussing women entrepreneurship in the Middle Eastern context." According to the research of Salama (2020) this remained a problem some 8 years later but in addition to the lack of research and data the MENA region is found to face specific barriers and constraints for women. These are:

- Gender specific barriers
- Cultural norms
- Civil Law
- Access to financial services and resources
- The Business Environment

How such barriers operate in each of the countries of the region remains unclear so the in-depth country analyses that this book provides will be welcomed by all those with an interest in the region, in entrepreneurship, in female entrepreneurship and in the role of women in the economy and society. Hence, *Women Entrepreneurs in North Africa* is a much needed antidote to the lack of research and data on a topic that is of vital importance not just to the future economic and social development of the region, but to the well-being of women and the global economy.

References

Brush, C. (1997), "Women Entrepreneurs: The Way Forward," in S. Birley and D. F. Muzyka, eds., *Mastering Entrepreneurship: The Complete MBA Companion in Entrepreneurship,* London, United Kingdom: Pearson Education.

Global Entrepreneurship Monitor (2019), *2018/2019 Women's Entrepreneurship Report,* London, United Kingdom: Global Entrepreneurship Research Association.

Hattab, H. (2012), "Toward Understanding Female Entrepreneurship in Middle Eastern and North African Countries. A Cross Country Comparison of Female Entrepreneurship. *Education, Business and Society: Contemporary Middle Eastern Issues* 5 (3), pp. 171–186.

Mintzberg, H. (1973), *The Nature of Managerial Work,* New York, NY: Harper & Row.

Salama, H. (2020), *Women Entrepreneurship in MENA: An Analysis,* EcoMENA. https://www.ecomena.org/women-entrepreneurship-in-mena/

Syeed, N., and Zafar, R. (2014), *Arab Women Rising: 35 Entrepreneurs Making a Difference in the Arab World. Knowledge @wharton,* Philadelphia, PA: University of Pennsylvania.

© 2022 World Scientific Publishing Company
https://doi.org/10.1142/9789811236600_fmatter

Foreword by Professor Candida Brush

Franklin W. Olin Professor in Entrepreneurship, Babson College, USA
Visiting Adjunct, Dublin City University, Ireland & Nord University,
Norway

Who are the women entrepreneurs launching and growing businesses North Africa? What do we know about these women entrepreneurs? These questions provide a strong motivation for this investigation into women's entrepreneurship, which is long overdue.

Globally, 252 million women around the world are entrepreneurs and another 153 million women are operating established businesses, according to the Global Entrepreneurship Monitor 2018/2019 Report on Women's Entrepreneurship (Elam et al., 2019). Within the Middle East North Africa (MENA) Region, TEA activities are lower (at 9%) compared to the other regions, but within this region, countries like Angola and show equal rates of TEA for men and women. Further, women in the MENA are more likely to be motivated out of necessity (32%) other parts of the world except Sub Saharan Africa (42.1%). But, importantly, the percentage of men motivated by necessity is less than 1.6% than for men which is one of the lowest gaps across regions. In addition, the gap between men and women in entrepreneurial intentions is very low, 39.2% for men and 36.6% for men. In other words, there is evidence that entrepreneurial activity among women entrepreneurs is moving forward and, and, while there remains a gender gap, there is progress.

However, research on women's entrepreneurship has focused primarily on samples of North American and Western European women entrepreneurs. While research on women's entrepreneurship comprises overall, less than 10–15% of all entrepreneurial studies (Greene and Brush, 2021; Jennings and Brush, 2013) those examining women entrepreneurs and their businesses from North Africa are quite few, and research is fragmented (Bastian et al., 2018). This is a concern for a couple of reasons; first, the tendency is to apply "western-centric" models to research approaches, which means we may miss crucial aspects of understanding or misunderstand approaches, models and business practices of these women entrepreneurs. Second, when differences to the western-centric models are discovered, this positions women entrepreneurs from other regions as different, or in some cases at a deficit. By following a western-centric model we may be missing the elaboration of new approaches and new insights in to women's entrepreneurship not only in this region, but generally.

Another challenge is that current literature about women's entrepreneurship in the MENA region tends to focus on the "barriers" or challenges related to context, culture, institutions, stereotypes and business practices (Halkias et al., 2011; Laffineur et al., 2018). This is not surprising because the barriers and challenges are numerous and greater than for other regions. However, it is also important to explore the contributions of women entrepreneurs, their success and their models to gain a full picture of their participation in entrepreneurship in this region.

I am pleased that this volume will focus on a variety of countries about which we have less information about women's entrepreneurship generally, and collectively, it will tell a more complete story of women's entrepreneurship in North Africa. The authors have taken the time to dig deep into the context for each of the countries considered, Morocco, Algeria, Tunisia, Libya, Egypt and Sudan providing an historical overview, current state and a perspective on the future. The future perspective for each of these countries gives us very high hopes for entrepreneurship generally, for women's entrepreneurship specifically and for women's entrepreneurship in North Africa most particularly!

References

Bastian, B. L., Y. M. Sidani, and Y. El Amine (2018), "Women Entrepreneurship in the Middle East and North Africa: A Review of Knowledge Areas and Research Gaps," *Gender in Management* 33 (1), pp. 14–29. https://doi.org/10.1108/GM-07-2016-0141

Elam, A., C. G. Brush, P. G. Greene, B. Baumer, M. Dean, and R. Heavlow (2019). *Global Entrepreneurship Monitor 2018–2019 Women's Entrepreneurship Report*, London, United Kingdom: Global Entrepreneurship Research Association

Greene, P., and C. Brush (2021), "A Narrative Policy Analysis of Women's Entrepreneurship Across Micro, Meso and Macro Levels," in C. Henry, S. Coleman, K. Lewis, and L. Foss, eds., *Women's Entrepreneurship*

Policy: A Global Perspective, Northhampton, MA: Edward Elgar Publishing.

Halkias, D., C. Nwajiumba, N. Harkiolakis, and S. Caracatsanis (2011), "Challenges Facing Women Entrepreneurs in Nigeria," *Management Research Review* 34 (2), pp. 221–225.

Jennings, J. E., and C. G. Brush (2013), "Research on Women Entrepreneurs: Challenges to (and From) the Broader Entrepreneurship Literature?" *The Academy of Management Annals* 7, pp. 661–713.

Laffineur, C., M. Tavakoli, A. Fayolle, N. Amara, and M. Carco (2018), "Insights From Female Entrepreneurs in MENA Countries: Barriers and Success Factors," in N. Faghih and M. Zali, eds., *Entrepreneurship Ecosystem in the Middle East and North Africa (MENA). Contributions to Management Science,* Cham: Springer. https://doi.org/10.1007/978-3-319-75913-5_12

© 2022 World Scientific Publishing Company
https://doi.org/10.1142/9789811236600_fmatter

Foreword by Professor Shaker Zahra

The women of North Africa have long been known for their courage and bravery; many of them have been leaders in their countries' wars of independence and their struggle for equality. They also have a long history of entrepreneurialism. Indeed, centuries ago, Ibn Khaldoun wrote about this entrepreneurial spirit, explaining it as natural response to the external environment in which these women lived. Entrepreneurial activities, thus, manifested an attempt to address the challenges found in the environment as well as take advantage of nature's bountiful gifts and resources. In this conception, entrepreneurship by north Africa's women represents a deliberate effort to improve quality of life and improve wealth.

North Africa's countries have experienced long periods of colonialism. During this dark period, colonists have attempted to obliterate prevailing cultures and social structures, even local languages. Yet, after decades of struggle, these countries emerged independent and victorious. And for the past few decades, they have focused on promoting entrepreneurial activities, especially among and by women. This push has coincided with a region-wide effort to recognize women's rights more. This is why this is an important book: it takes stock of where these efforts stand today, how much progress has been made, and how much more needs to be done. Especially important, when we take the various chapters of this book together, we gain important insights into what makes women entrepreneurship in North Africa different from other parts of the world, even though these women continue to encounter many of the same obstacles observed everywhere.

Clearly, this is an interesting and timely book about an important region of the world. The same women who have shown courage in the wars of their countries' independence are now demonstrating the same spirit in their entrepreneurial pursuits. The book provides an interesting and compelling portrait of these different entrepreneurial activities. The editors have done a masterful job in putting together an authoritative book that will add richly to the field. I hope you enjoy reading the book and learning about this important part of the world.

Shaker A. Zahra
Robert E. Buuck Chair of entrepreneurship
University of Minnesota

© 2022 World Scientific Publishing Company
https://doi.org/10.1142/9789811236600_fmatter

Editorial Board

Sucheta AGARWAL	GLA University, India
Osnat AKIRAV	Western Galilee College, Israel
Hanane BENADDI	Ibn Tofail University, Morocco
Didier CHABOT	La Sorbonne, France
Naima CHERCHEM	Ryerson University, Canada
Meghna CHHABRA	Manav Rachna International Institute of Research and Studies, India
Raphael H. COHEN	University of Geneva, Switzerland
David CRAWFORD	Department of Sociology and Anthropology at Fairfield University, USA
Aliaa EL SHOUBAKI	Prague University of Economics and Business, Czech Republic
Maria ELO	University of Southern Denmark
Hamid ETEMAD	McGill University, Canada
Fethi FERHANE	Director for Algeria, Evidencia Business Academy
Bella GALPERIN	University of Tampa, USA
Elisa GIACOSA	Università degli Studi di Torino, Italy
Hala HATTAB	British University in Egypt
Robert HISRICH	Kent State University, USA
Gözde İNAL-CAVLAN	European University of Lefke, Northern Cyprus

Diala KABBARA	University of Pavia, Italy
Samppa KAMARA	University of Oulu, Finland
Christian KEEN	Université Laval, Canada
George LODORFOS	Leeds Business School, UK
Amandine MAUS	Aix-Marseille Université, France
Kamel MOULAI	Faculté d'Economie et de Gestion UMM Tizi Ouzou, Algeria
Amina OMRANE	University of Sfax, Tunisia
Rebecca OSAMUDIAME	Dalhousie University, Canada
Aidin SALAMZADEH	University of Tehran, Iran
Naman SHARMA	Indian Institute of Foreign Trade, India
Ekaterina VOROBEVA	Bremen International Graduate School of Social Sciences, Germany
Hedi YEZZA	Université de Sherbrooke, Canada
Iman Samir YOUSSEF	Newgiza University, Egypt

© 2022 World Scientific Publishing Company
https://doi.org/10.1142/9789811236600_fmatter

Preface

As I was growing up, in Canada, Arabic was the language most spoken at home, and my parents had many friends from across North Africa. I grew up Canadian by nationality, complemented by considerable cultural capital that was Arab in origin. I was raised with tremendous affection for the people of North Africa—encompassing Morocco, Algeria, Tunisia, Libya, Egypt and Sudan.

Descendants of pre-Arab inhabitants of North Africa, the indigenous people of this region are the Berbers — present here since the dawn of recorded history. With Pharaonic origins, the Copts have also been in Egypt well before the arrival of Islam; like the Berbers, they do not have Arab origins. Relatively recently, during the 7th century, Arabs from Western Asia (see Dana et al., 2022) introduced Islam here, spreading their language and prompting the Islamisation of North Africa.

I remember the excitement when I was a child and we received a letter from my mother's uncle in Casablanca; the envelopes always had a large stamp featuring King Mohammed V. This uncle was born in Iraq but chose Morocco as the place to be. Faraway, I read about narrow streets (Exhibit P.1), fortified villages (see Exhibit P.2), and bazaars (Exhibit P.3) of this lovely kingdom.

I read about all of the seven countries that the United Nations considered to comprise as North Africa: Algeria, Egypt (known as the United Arab Republic from 1958 to 1971, including Syria until 1961 and the occupied Gaza Strip until 1967), Libya, Morocco, Sudan, Tunisia and Spanish Sahara, now merged into Morocco. While fascinated with their differences, I also noted a commonality — the role of women, with a status different than men (Exhibit P.4).

Exhibit P.1 Rush hour; photograph © Léo-Paul Dana

Exhibit P.2 Aït Benhaddou along a former caravan route; photograph © Léo-Paul Dana

Exhibit P.3 Spices at bazaar; photograph © Léo-Paul Dana

Exhibit P.4 Unlike men; photograph © Léo-Paul Dana

The map looked quite different during the 1890s (see Exhibit P.5), when my maternal grandmother came to the British-occupied[1] Khedivate of Egypt[2] on camel-back, from Ottoman Iraq. In Cairo, my grandmother married an entrepreneur with Persian roots. They raised their eight children in Heliopolis, and there my mother learned the importance of trade — and marvels such as the Suez Canal (Exhibit P.6). My mother recalled that by 1929 KLM was flying from Amsterdam to Cairo and from Cairo to Baghdad and on to the Dutch East Indies (that became Indonesia after WWII). Technology was replacing caravans, but the role of women in society had yet to evolve. As a teenager my mother lived with her unmarried aunt, who was a self-employed seamstress — neither a lucrative nor socially-desirable occupation in a society in which single women were looked down upon. They were so poor that the best they could afford was to reside on a roof-top; they lived, with no electricity, on the roof-top of the Khedive Ismail Building (Exhibit P.7) — named for Ismail Pasha (1830–1895), Ottoman viceroy of the Khedivate of Egypt.

My father moved to Egypt with his parents; at home in Alexandria, the family spoke Italian, but he soon mastered Arabic — a lovely language and the one of my earliest recollections. Egypt was already home to a large Italian community when the family arrived in 1925. Sixty years later, in Egypt, I discovered that the longest established Italian family in Egypt was Jewish and traced its origins to Leghorn from where they arrived in 1815; I was told that to escape 19th century religious persecution in Italy, Jewish Italians came to Egypt, a much more tolerant place. Many Italians also arrived from Libya, which Italy took over from the Ottoman Empire in 1911 and colonised until WWII (see Exhibit P.8). In 1940, the Italian army attacked Egypt and British authorities came to intern my grandfather because — like other Italians in Egypt — he was suspected of co-operating with the Nazis. Intervention by an Egyptian friend of my father caused the immediate release of my grandfather.

In Egypt, sympathy for Italians was so strong that, in 1946, when King Vittorio Emanuele III abdicated from the Italian throne, he was invited to reside in Alexandria. By that time, my grandfather's seven children were of working age; all of the boys became entrepreneurs, but it was made clear that for the girls it was not socially desirable to be self-employed.

---

[1] The United Kingdom had invaded the Ottoman Khedivate of Egypt in 1882.

[2] The Khedivate of Egypt remained a state of the Ottoman Empire until 1914 when the United Kingdom established the Sultanate of Egypt, a British protectorate that lasted until 1922.

Exhibit P.5 Photo of *The Century Atlas* map from 1897; photograph © Léo-Paul Dana

Exhibit P.6 The Suez Canal; photograph © Léo-Paul Dana

Exhibit P.7 Khedive Ismail Building, Cairo; photograph © Léo-Paul Dana

Exhibit P.8 Showing Italian presence in Africa; photograph © Léo-Paul Dana

Exhibit P.9 Men are present everywhere; photograph © Léo-Paul Dana

Exhibit P.10 Dealing in textiles at Mahalla el-Kubra; photograph © Léo-Paul Dana

Exhibit P.11 Possibly an entrepreneur in the future; photograph
© Léo-Paul Dana

Although my parents left Egypt in 1951, they never stopped talking about how well people got along there, living harmoniously and helping each other thrive in business. Egypt was very multicultural, and my parents spoke of friends who were Armenian Orthodox, and others who were Copts, Greek Orthodox, Italian Catholics, Jews and Muslims. My mother would tell me that everybody participated in everyone else's festivals. One of my uncles spoke of going to the same school as King Farouk. My mother would tell me about dining with the king, and my father would talk about going to mosque with Farouk.

An economically prosperous area, North Africa today generates a third of Africa's total GDP. What is known about its women entrepreneurs of the 21st century? Indeed, men dominate much economic activity (Exhibit P.9), but women entrepreneurs are also busy (Exhibit P.10), and young women are considering self-employment (Exhibit P.11). Contributions in this volume investigate the phenomenon of women entrepreneurs from the Atlantic Ocean to the Red Sea.

Reference

Dana, L.P., A. Salamzadeh, V. Ramadani, and R. Palalić (2022), *Understanding Contexts of Business in Western Asia: Land of Bazaars and High-Tech Booms,* Singapore: World Scientific.

Léo-Paul Dana
Dalhousie University
Chaire ETI–Sorbonne Business School, Université Paris 1
Panthéon-Sorbonne

© 2022 World Scientific Publishing Company
https://doi.org/10.1142/9789811236600_fmatter

Editors

Léo-Paul Dana is Professor at Dalhousie University and holds titles of Professor at Montpellier Business School and Visiting Professor at Kingston University. He is associated with the Chaire ETI at Sorbonne Business School. A graduate of McGill University and HEC-Montreal, he has served as Marie Curie Fellow at Princeton University and Visiting Professor at INSEAD. He has published extensively in a variety of journals including: *Entrepreneurship: Theory & Practice, International Business Review, International Small Business Journal, Journal of Business Research, Journal of Small Business Management, Journal of World Business, Small Business Economics,* and *Technological Forecasting & Social Change.*

Dina Nziku is a lecturer in the School of Business and Enterprise at the University of the West of Scotland (UWS), Paisley Campus. She has a particular interest on female entrepreneurship and government strategies/policies for promoting enterprise and innovation in developing countries. Dina also works with ethnic minority women groups as well as inspiring youths in Glasgow. She has published papers in academic journals such as: *The Journal of Women Entrepreneurship and Education,* and has presented a number of research papers at various international conferences and within the United Kingdom. Dina has also made a number of keynote speeches at conferences, such as the Think Tank-International Conference on Women Entrepreneurship and has taken part in the United Nations (UNCTAD) Panel: "Multi-year Expert Meeting on Investment, Innovation and Entrepreneurship for Productive Capacity-Building and Sustainable Development" where Dina was invited to speak on Sub-Saharan Female Entrepreneurship.

Ramo Palalić is an Assistant Professor at the Management Department, College of Economics and Political Science, Sultan Qaboos University, Oman. His research is in the area of entrepreneurship, leadership, and management. Dr. Palalić has authored and co-authored many articles in globally recognised journals like *Management Decision, International Journal of Entrepreneurial Behavior & Research, International Entrepreneurship and Management Journal*, and alike. Additionally, he has co-authored/co-edited several books and many book chapters in the field of business and entrepreneurship published with internationally prominent publishers (Springer, Routledge, World Scientific). Moreover, Dr. Palalić is serving as the reviewer/editor board member in several well-established international journals. Apart from his research, he was involved in business projects in the areas of entrepreneurial leadership and marketing management, in private and public organisations.

Veland Ramadani is a Professor of Entrepreneurship and Family Business at Faculty of Business and Economics, South East European University, North Macedonia. His research interests include entrepreneurship, small business management and family businesses. He authored or co-authored around 140 research articles, 11 textbooks and 18 edited books. He has published in *Journal of Business Research, International Entrepreneurship and Management Journal, International Journal of Entrepreneurial Behavior & Research, Technological Forecasting and Social Change*, among others. Dr. Ramadani is co-Editor-in-Chief of Journal of Enterprising Communities (JEC). He has received the Award for Excellence 2016 — Outstanding Paper by Emerald Group Publishing. In 2017, he was appointed as a member of Supervisory Board of Development Bank of North Macedonia, where for ten months served as an acting Chief Operating Officer (COO) as well.

© 2022 World Scientific Publishing Company
https://doi.org/10.1142/9789811236600_0001

Chapter 1

Indigenous Women in North Africa: Amazigh Women and Argan Oil

A. Allan Degen

Ben-Gurion University of the Negev, Beer Sheva, Israel

Abstract

The argan tree is endemic to southwestern Morocco. For centuries, Amazigh women, many of whom are monolingual (speaking only Tamazight), illiterate and innumerate, have been producing argan oil from the fruit of the tree for culinary and medicinal purposes. The whole process was done manually and included harvesting the fruit from the ground, removing the outer pulp and peel to expose the nut, cracking the nut with a pounder (stone) to obtain usually one but up to three kernels, roasting the kernels if for culinary purposes — not so, if for cosmetic purposes, grinding the kernels in a millstone, kneading the ground kernels and extracting the oil. Because of the exotic 'hazelnut' taste and beneficial health properties, the oil has become a very expensive commodity worldwide, selling between $300 and $400 a litre. Labelled as 'liquid gold', it is reputed to delay ageing and hair loss and to prevent or treat a large variety of diseases. Argan oil cooperatives, employing only women, were initiated in 1996. This was considered a win-win situation as it would protect and conserve the fragile argan forests and provide work and salaries for Amazigh women, an impoverished group in a highly restrictive patriarchal society. The women were entitled to voting rights and a share of the annual profits, in addition to literacy classes, health services and child care. Except for the cracking of the nuts, all steps in the production of the oil became mechanised. There are mixed reports on the benefits, earnings and status of the women in the cooperatives. Control of argan oil, which was exclusively in the hands of Amazigh women, has been usurped by the state and businessmen. Today, 99% of the argan forests are publically owned. In

the production of argan oil, approximately 95% of the women only crack
nuts in the traditional manner.

Morocco — Geography and Demographics

Morocco (Arabic: المغرب; al-maḡrib — means place the sun sets; the west;
Tamazight: ⵍⵎⵖⵔⵉⴱ; lmeɣrib), with Rabat as the capital, is located in the
Maghreb region of North Africa. The country is bordered by Algeria to the
east and Western Sahara to the south, and has a long coastline on
the Mediterranean Sea in the north and the Atlantic Ocean in the West
(Exhibit 1.1). Morocco covers 446,550 km^2 of undisputed territory (between
latitudes 27° and 36°N, and longitudes 1° and 14°W) or 710,850 km^2
(between 21° and 36°N, and 1° and 17°W), if the disputed territories, mainly
Western Sahara, are included. The landscape of Morocco is very varied and
includes large mountain ranges and desert. The Atlas Mountains extend

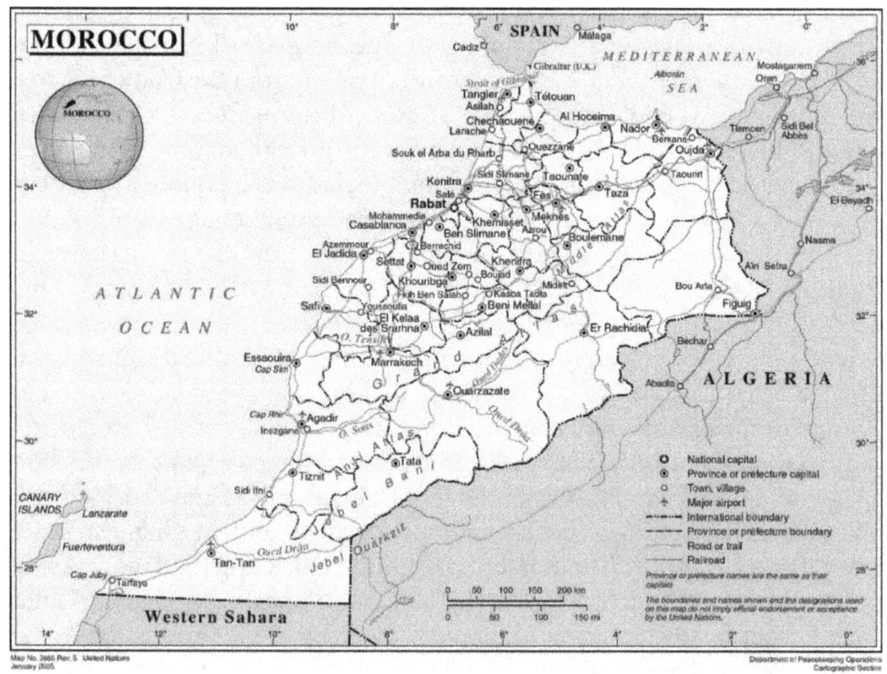

Exhibit 1.1 Map of Morocco

Source: United Nations, Map No. 3686, Rev. 5 (used with permission).

from the northeast to the southwest of the country, while the Rif Mountains border the Mediterranean from the northwest to the northeast. The vast Sahara Desert covers much of the southeast part of the country.

Morocco became a protectorate of France in 1912 with the Treaty of Fez and gained independence in 1956. Mohammed V reigned as king from 1957 and, following his death, Hussan II succeeded him from 1961. It was during his reign that the first general elections were held in 1963. Mohammed VI followed Hussan II to the throne and has been king since 1999. The king acts as both the secular political leader and the 'Commander of the Faithful', as a direct descendant of the Prophet Mohammed (MSN Encarta, 2009).

There were approximately 37,000,000 people in Morocco in 2020 (Knoema, 2020). Of the total, 99% were considered Arab-Berbers (Arabic: العرب والبربر *al-'arab wa-l-barbar*), an ethno-linguistic group of mixed Arab and Berber origin, most of whom speak a variant of Maghrebi Arabic as their native language. Over 98% of Moroccan residents are Muslim, the official religion of the country — mainly Sunnis and less than 0.1% Shias — slightly under 1% are Christians, and there are small populations of Jews and Baha'is. Arabic, spoken by 98% of the population, and Tamazight, spoken by 43% of the population, are the official languages of Morocco, Tamazight being added recently in 2011 (Agence France-Presse, 2020). The French language (63% of the population) is spoken widely in Morocco, while English (14%) and Spanish (10%) are also used but to a much lesser extent.

Since 1993, the country has followed a policy of privatisation of a number of economic sectors, which were previously controlled by the government. In 2019, the gross domestic product (GDP) in terms of purchasing power parity (PPP), which reflects differences in the cost of living and inflation rates of the countries, totaled $332.4 billion, averaged $9339 per capita and was ranked fifth in Africa; whereas, the nominal GDP totaled $122.5 billion and averaged $3441 per capita (IMF, 2020). Services account for over 50% of the GDP and industry, particularly tourism, accounts for an additional 25%. In 2019, Morocco had a Human Development Index (HDI) of 0.686, considered medium level, but ranked 121st of 189 measured countries and lowest of the North African countries, and, in 2015, had a Gini index of 40.3, also considered a medium rank. HDI is a composite index that includes life expectancy, education and per capita income while the Gini index represents the income or wealth inequality within a nation. Agriculture is the largest employer in Morocco, with about 40% of the work force. Rain-fed grains, mainly barley and wheat, are grown without irrigation in the northwest of the country. Irrigation, mainly from artesian wells, is used to grow olives, citrus fruits, and wine grapes on the Atlantic coast. Livestock is produced throughout the country and there is fishing along the coast, in particular at Agadir, Essaouira, El Jadida and Larache (ADD, 2018; HDR, 2020; IMF, 2020).

Imazighen

Imazighen (Tamazight: ⵥⵍⴲⵅⵤⵓⵉ, ⵍⵅⵙⵍ,: singular: Amaziɣ, ⵍⵅⵤⵓ ⵍⵅⵙ), meaning free or noble people, are an ethnic group indigenous to northwest Africa, speaking the Amazigh languages of the Afro-Asiatic family. They are also known as 'Berbers', a name disliked by the Imazighen. The word Berbers originated from the Greek *barbario* and the Latin *barbarus* from which Arabs derived the term 'barbariy', meaning primitive or foreign. It meant 'babble' or 'nonsense' to the Romans and referred to non-Romans whose speech was intelligible. A barbarous was a barbarian who was different and inferior to the Romans (Hoffman, 2008).

There are records of the Amazigh people in North Africa dating back to before 10,000 BC (Tampa Bay Times, 2016). The area which they inhabited was invaded and ruled by a succession of powers including the Saharans, Phoenicians, Greeks, Romans, Vandals and Byzantines. The Imazighen were able to resist these invasions and maintain their cultural practices, language and religious beliefs. Traditionally, the Imazighen, who are identified through tribal affiliations, were animists, while many adopted Christianity or Judaism during the Roman rule. In the late 7th century, with the explosive spread of Islam by Arabs from the East, the Imazighen gradually assimilated as Sunni Muslims. The Arab invaders took control of the cities, forcing the Imazighen to retreat to the mountainous regions of Morocco (Maddy-Weitzman, 2006). However, the Imazighen maintained their identity separate from the Arabs, and four Sunni Imazighen dynasties, the Almoravids, Almohads, Marinids and Wattasids, ruled Morocco from 1060 to 1549. The Arab Saadi dynasty ruled from 1549, followed by the Alaouite dynasty in 1666, which still rules today. Ottoman invaders attempted to conquer Morocco, but Morocco was the only Arab country not to fall under Ottoman rule.

Imazighen were generally sedentary farmers and shepherds, although the Tuareg (blue people) and Zenaga, two Amazigh groups, were nomadic in the southern Sahara, and some groups, such as the Chaouis, practiced transhumance. Besides agriculture, Imazighen were also merchants, using camel caravans to transport goods, traders and shopkeepers. Today, trade is generally at a subsistence level and through personal relations, and is often centred around the bazaar (Dana, 2006). Imazighen live in the mountains in the Rif, Middle Atlas, High Atlas and Anti Atlas regions and in smaller settlements throughout North Africa. There are approximately 36 million Imazighen worldwide and, in Africa, are distributed from western Egypt to the Canary Islands and from the Mediterranean coast to deep into the Sahara (Peabody Museum, 2021). Largest populations in Africa are in Morocco (19 million) and Tunisia (13 million), with smaller numbers in Niger (1 million), Mali (0.7 million), Libya (0.55 million), Tunisia (0.1 million), Egypt (0.02 million), Mauritania (0.005 million), Canary Islands and Burkina Faso. In addition, there are approximately 2.4 million Imazighen in western Europe, mainly in France and Spain, and this number has been increasing in recent years. It is estimated that over 40% of the Moroccan population is Amazigh and approximately 80% has Amazigh ancestral origins (Maddy-Weitzman, 2006; New World Encyclopedia, 2019).

There are still traces of Berber Jews in Morocco today. It is thought that the Berber Jews originated from Jews who arrived in Morocco after the destruction of the first temple by the Babylonians in 586 BC. Many of these Jews settled in the Anti-Atlas region among the Amazigh tribes. They were not farmers but were businessmen and had cordial relations with Imazighen. In later years, they co-existed on excellent terms with the Amazigh Muslims, and often acted as mediators in business dealings between Imazighen and Arabs (Dana and Dana, 2008). However, with the creation of the State of Israel in 1948, Morocco joined the Arab block in condemning Israel. Anti-Jewish violence broke out, and Moroccan Jews, including Berber Jews, fled mainly to Israel. Today, Berber Jews in Israel still speak fondly of Morocco and visit the country often. In turn, many Imazighen remember the good relations with the Jews and support the State of Israel (Schwartz, 2019; Barnett, 2020).

The inclusion of Tamazight as an official language followed strong demonstrations for equal rights and for the preservation of the Amazigh culture and language (El Aissati, 2005; Schwartz, 2019). The recognition of the Tamazight language led to the Tifinagh alphabet appearing on public notices, along with Arabic and French, and the inclusion of the language in the educational system. The language is primarily oral, although it has been written for at least 2,500 years and has three main dialects: Central Atlas Tamazight in Central Morocco, Tarifit, in the Rif, and Tashelhit in the south, which includes the High Atlas, Anti-Atlas, plain of the Souss and the Sahara (Belahsen et al., 2017).

Imazighen are a patriarchal society with strong segregations between genders. As head of the household, the man is the decision-maker in the family and can sit in the *djemââ*, a tribal council that decides issues related to community life. The husband is the money earner and, under Moudawana law (Moroccan family law), is legally required to support his wife (Charrad, 2012). This law gives the man the right to decide whether his wife can appear in public and restricts women from deciding on how household income should be spent, if she receives adequate clothing, food and housing (Bordat et al., 2011). Many Amazigh women are monolingual, speaking only Tamazight, illiterate and innumerate. In some rural areas, the illiteracy rate for women is close to 90% and fewer than 15% of the girls are enrolled in secondary school (UNDP, 2018). The main role of Amazigh women is to raise many children and prepare and serve meals. She is responsible for the house and family, and for the children's health, education and welfare. Women also participate in small-scale farming, tending livestock and growing vegetables. It is socially acceptable for women to earn money in the privacy of the home by such work as cooking, baking, henna painting for weddings and parties, sewing, cleaning nearby houses and selling small items to other women of the community (Perry et al., 2019).

The majority of working age Amazigh men have left the household in search of work, either locally or abroad, and send money to support the family. These men have learned Arabic and integrated into Moroccan lifestyle. Consequently, women left behind not only handle their traditional roles but are also burdened with additional work that was done by men.In essence, the women have preserved Amazigh traditions, culture and language. One of these traditions was the production of argan oil from the fruit of argan trees. Income from the sale of Argan oil was considered 'women's money', which could be used for domestic goods, school fees and personal items.

Argan Trees and Argan Oil

The Argan tree (*Argania spinose* (L.) Skeels), known as the 'Tree of Life', is endemic to south-west Morocco in semi-arid and arid regions (Exhibit 1.2). The tree grows mainly in the Sous Massa region, bordered by the Atlas Mountains in the East, in the provinces of Agadir, Taroudant, Essaouira and Tiznit. It has been difficult to domesticate argan trees, but the temperate ocean climate and wind protection from the mountains provide optimum conditions for their growth (Kenny and DeZborowski,

Exhibit 1.2 Argan trees in arid and semi-arid areas in southwestern Morocco;
photograph © GIZ/Tristan Vostry (with permission).

2007). The deep root system of the argan tree allows its survival in drought-prone areas and also protects the area against soil erosion and against encroachment by the Sahara Desert (Lybbert, 2007). There are approximately 21 million argan trees, covering an area of close to 1 million hectares (Mounir et al., 2015); however, the number of trees has been declining. The density of the forests declined by approximately 45% between 1970 and 2007 (le Polain de Waroux and Lambin, 2011; le Polain de Waroux, 2013) due to increasing aridity, over-grazing by livestock, land conversion to commercial crops, urban encroachment and the demand for firewood and wood for construction (Lybbert et al., 2010; Ruas et al., 2015). To protect and conserve the trees, the argan forest was designated an UNESCO biosphere reserve in 1998 (UNESCO, 2002), and 500 hectares were reforested in 2005, 2200 hectares in 2009 and 100,000 hectares in 2017.

The slow-growing, spiny Argan tree reaches a height of 10 metres and can live more than 200 years (Exhibit 1.3). This tree starts to produce fruit after 5 years, produces approximately 10 kg per year and reaches maximum production capacity after 20 years. The hermaphrodite greenish-yellow or white flowers appear between May or June. Fruit require more than a year

Exhibit 1.3 Argan tree in southwestern Morocco; photograph © Valérie Heuzé, Feedipedia, www.feedipedia.org (with permission).

to mature, ripening in June to July of the following year, when they fall and are harvested from the ground. The fruit, an oval berry the size and shape of a large olive, is 2 to 4 centimetres in length, 1.5 to 3 centimetres in width, and weighs 5 to more than 20 grams (Exhibits 1.4 and 1.5). Goats climb the trees adeptly and consume leaves and fruit (Exhibit 1.6). The hard nut of the fruit cannot be digested and is excreted via the faeces.

Exhibit 1.4 Argan tree with ripe fruit in southwestern Morocco; photograph ©
Valérie Heuzé, Feedipedia, www.feedipedia.org (with permission).

The argan tree serves as a source of wood for building, firewood and
charcoal, fodder for livestock, shade (Alados & El Aich, 2008) and the fruit
is used to produce argan oil for culinary, medicinal and cosmetic purposes
(Lybbert et al., 2010; Charrouf and Guillaume, 2018). The argan forest is
governed through tenure agreements called *agdal* rights, which permit
households to collect fruit during the harvesting season, from June to

Exhibit 1.5 Ripe fruit from the argan tree; photograph © Valérie Heuzé, Feedipedia, www.feedipedia.org (with permission).

Exhibit 1.6 Goats climb the argan tree and consume leaves and fruit; photograph © Sheila Warshawsky (with permission).

August 12 (Charrouf et al., 2011). These rights are usually inherited and are rarely sold. During the off-season, the argan forest is divided among villages and the forest dwellers can access and use the forest through *azroug* rights, which are held by the residents of the villages. There are also private argan trees owned by households (Ilhiane, 1999; Lybbert et al., 2010; ODCO, 2020).

For centuries, exclusively Amazigh women, in particular the Tashelhit speaking women of the Souss, have produced argan oil manually from argan fruit; copper-coloured oil with a slight hazelnut flavour for culinary purposes and golden-coloured oil for cosmetic/medicinal purposes (Charrouf and Guillaume, 2008, 2009; Ruas et al., 2015). Culinary oil was used on salads, on couscous and for making a popular Amazigh spread called *amlou*, which consists of argan oil, honey and almonds. Cosmetic/medicinal oil was used to treat various ailments, including, dry skin, acne, psoriasis, eczema, joint pain and skin inflammation and to prevent wrinkles, hair loss and dry hair (Charrouf et al., 2008; Guillaume and Charrouf, 2011). In the preparation of argan oil, several Amazigh women usually participate in the process together, singing and sharing the workload. The fallen, ripe fruits are collected from the ground (Exhibits 1.7 and 1.8),

Exhibit 1.7 Amazigh women collecting argan fruit from the ground; photograph © GIZ/Tristan Vostry (with permission).

Exhibit 1.8 Argan fruit collected by Amazigh women;
photograph © GIZ/Tristan Vostry (with permission).

air-dried in clay containers for approximately 10 days, and the outer layer (pulp and peel) is de-pulped to remove the nut (Exhibits 1.9 and 1.10). Next is the arduous, labour-intensive task of cracking open the nut (Exhibit 1.11). The woman holds a pounder in one hand and the nut between the thumb and index finger on an anvil (*affiach*) in the other hand, and then 'pounds' the nut (Exhibit 1.12). Each cracked nut provides usually one, but up to two or three, small, white kernels (Exhibit 1.13). When argan oil is prepared for culinary purposes, the kernels are roasted lightly on clay plates for 30 minutes to remove the anti-nutritive argenine (Cayuela et al., 2008). Argan shells usually produce the fire for the roasting. The roasted kernels are then ground in a homemade millstone (*azreg*) composed of a stationary bedstone and a cone-shaped runner stone, which has a handle to rotate the stone and a hole in the centre in which kernels are inserted (Exhibit 1.14). A brownish, viscous liquid is produced, which is mixed with lukewarm water and kneaded by hand for several minutes (Exhibit 1.15). This mixture gradually solidifies, releasing an emulsion from which argan oil is decanted and then filtered. It requires approximately 35 kg of dried fruits and 58 hours of work to produce 1 litre of argan oil (Exhibit 1.16). The residue remaining after the oil is collected is bitter,

Exhibit 1.9 Argan nuts ready to be cracked open; photograph © Valérie Heuzé, Feedipedia, www.feedipedia.org (with permission).

but nutritious, containing oil, proteins and carbohydrates, and, traditionally, is fed to livestock but can also be used in the making of soap. In the past, argan fruits were fed to goats, and the non-digestible nuts were collected from the faeces. However, this practice has stopped because of hygienic reasons and quality concerns, as the taste of the oil and its

Exhibit 1.10 Large range in size of nuts obtained from argan fruit; photograph © Nadav Solowey (with permission).

chemical composition were altered. The addition of water to the ground kernels is also a concern because of chemical and bacteriological contamination. The oil was, and still is in some cases, sold by the women's husbands and children on the side of the road or at local markets (Skog, 2013; Huang, 2017).

Exhibit 1.11 Women sitting and cracking argan nuts in the Akkain Ouargane Women's Cooperative; photograph © GIZ/Tristan Vostry (with permission).

There was little international interest in argan oil until the early 1990s. Oil production from traditional processing was sufficient to meet the demands for export (Argan Oil Direct, undated). However, reports on the healthy aspects transformed the oil into a highly desirable commodity — 'a super food, an anti-aging wonder, a miracle drug'. It was reputed to be an aromatherapy massage agent that harmonised, balanced, and relaxed the mind and body. Argan oil is very high in vitamin E, unsaturated fatty acids and low in saturated fatty acids (Cabrera-Vique et al., 2012). It contains high concentrations of tocopherols, CoQ10 and melatonin, which possess strong antioxidant capacities, and phytosterols, which reduce blood levels of low-density cholesterol (Norme SNIMA, 2003). Argan oil is reported to prevent cardiovascular, cerebrovascular and diabetes complications (Batta et al., 2016) and knee osteoarthritis (Essouiri et al., 2017). It improves the moisturising quality of the scalp and elasticity of the skin and prevents hair loss and aging of the skin.

Labelled as liquid gold, argan oil became a very expensive commodity. By 2006, there were an estimated 16 private cold-pressing plants built by foreign investors who sought to profit from argan oil. The plants produced a higher-quality oil with lower water content and longer shelf life at a lower price. Between 1999 and 2007, households selling argan oil doubled their

Exhibit 1.12 Amazigh woman holding a 'pounder' in the left hand and a kernel in the right hand after it was removed from the nut. Some kernels are on the anvil (*affiach*); photograph © Suzanne Jones, https://thetravelbunny.com/ (with permission).

Exhibit 1.13 Argan kernels collected from the nuts; photograph © Suzanne Jones, https://thetravelbunny.com/ (with permission).

Exhibit 1.14 Amazigh women grinding kernels using a millstone (*azreg*) in the Akkain Ouargane Women's Cooperative; photograph © GIZ/Tristan Vostry (with permission).

Exhibit 1.15 Ground kernels kneaded into a dough before extraction of oil; photograph © GIZ/Tristan Vostry (with permission).

production of oil tripled and the proportion of households selling fruit increased by sixfold. Collection of fruits became more aggressive, which led to numerous conflicts among the women (Lybbert et al., 2011). However only a small portion of the profits were earned by the Amazigh women and their increased collection of fruits was destructive to the argan trees in the longterm (Dossa, 2011). In addition, there were many cases of corrupt practices with argan oil; much of the oil sold to tourists was adulterated and women were being exploited and not receiving fair payment.

Professor Zoubida Charrouf, a Moroccan chemist who did much research on the composition and properties of argan oil, realised that changes had to be made in the production of argan oil. As part of the 'argan oil project' (AOP), which began in 1985, she planned to combine the preservation of the argan tree with the improvement of the social and economic status for Amazigh women. Amazigh women were the only people who were able to produce argan oil from fruit and, consequently, were indispensable to the enterprise. According to Charrouf and Guillaume (2018), for this enterprise to succeed, the AOP had to become more efficient and enact rigid quality controls. Five main changes were suggested: '1) argan oil production had to grow from family-scale to industrial-scale; 2) the argan

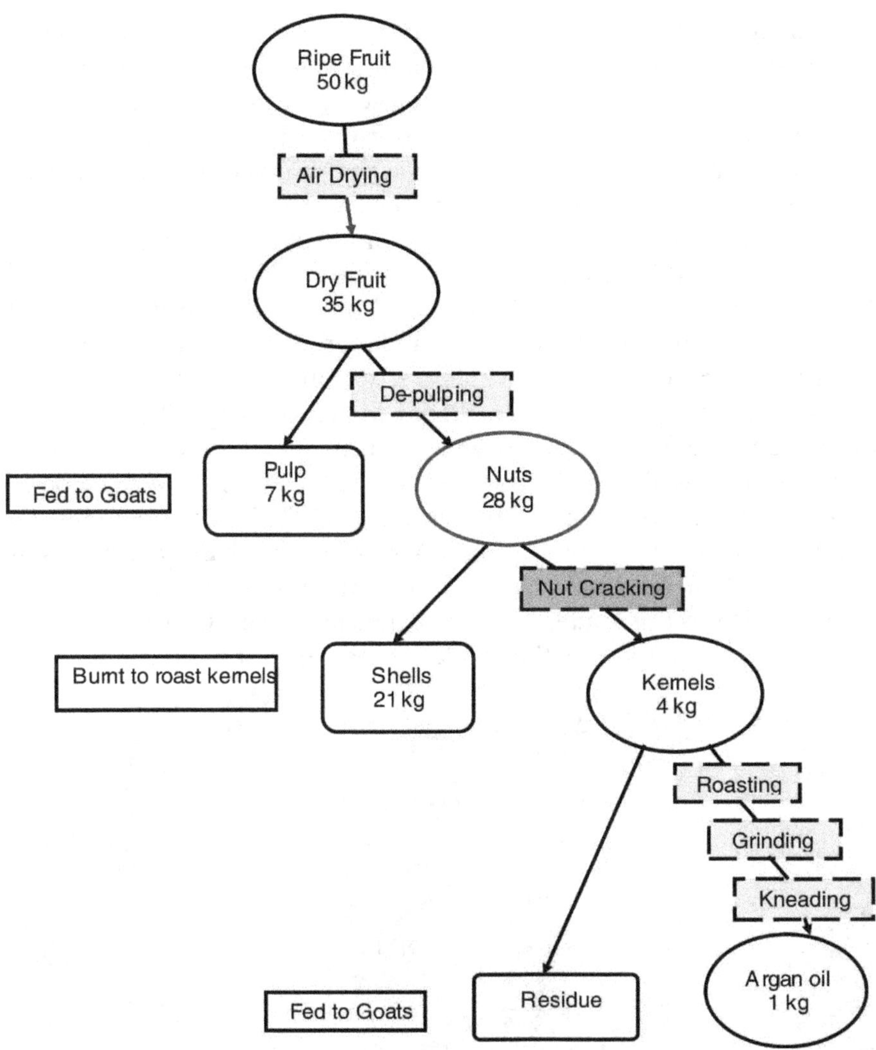

Exhibit 1.16 Production of argan oil from argan fruit. Only nut cracking has not been mechanised

oil composition had to be unambiguously established to avoid adulteration; 3) argan oil quality had to be certified; 4) the problem of argan oil low preservation had to be surmounted; and 5) for the project to be sustainable on the long-term, argan oil market had to be decoupled meaning that the virtues of the only-locally known argan oil had to become known well beyond the borders of Morocco.'

Changes in the process of argan oil production included mechanisation of some of the steps.For de-pulping, a machine with rough 'sand paper'-like plates was designed. Roasting kernels was improved and standardised by the use of gasburners or electric roasters (Aithammou et al., 2019), which resulted in a consistent taste and elimination of a burnt taste (Exhibit 1.17). Perhaps, the most important change was a machine to extract oil by cold pressing kernels at room temperature with no added water (Exhibit 1.18). This step increased the oil yield by 33% and decreased processing time by 50%. The elimination of water improved efficiency and produced an oil of high, standardised, and reproducible quality. Edible oil could be preserved for 2 years (Gharby et al., 2011) and cosmetic oil for 1 year (Gharby et al., 2014). Nut cracking was the only step not mechanised and could be done only by Amazigh women. Most of the fruit and/or nuts could be purchased from buyers (Perry, 2020). Attempts were made to design machines to crack the nut (Kisaala et al., 2010) and Robinson (2020) noted that there was some progress but that hand-cracking was still better than machine-cracking. This was important, according to Turner (2016), as this made women still indispensable. However, this may be just a matter of time, as the whole process, at least in Israel, has been

Exhibit 1.17 Woman operating an electric machine to roast kernels for culinary oil at the Akkain Ouargane Women's Cooperative; photograph © GIZ/Tristan Vostry (with permission).

Exhibit 1.18 A machine that grinds and extracts oil from argan kernels; photograph © Suzanne Jones, https://thetravelbunny.com/ (with permission).

mechanised, including the cracking of nuts by an Italian-made machine (Exhibit 1.19). It was suggested that should this occur in Morrocco, the Amazigh women might be eliminated from the production of the oil and regulated to just providing the fruit (le Polain de Waroux and Lambin, 2013).

Exhibit 1.19 Nut cracking machine manufactured in Italy and being used in Israel; photograph © Nadav Solowey (with permission).

Argan Oil Women's Cooperatives

Under the initiative of Charrouf, the first all-women's argan oil cooperative was established in 1996 at Amal, located in Tamanar, 70 kilometres south of Essaouira. It was difficult to recruit women because of the constrictions placed on them by their husbands; however, Charrouf managed to assemble 16 divorced or single women to join the cooperative (Charrouf et al., 2011). Once the women to earn money, more women joined and some husbands even asked for employment for their wives (Exhibit 1.20). The cooperatives were supported by non-governmental organisations (NGOs), government organisations and development practitioners. Two kinds of cooperatives were established (WIPO, undated): (1) non-mechanised cooperatives sponsored by the Deutsche Gesellschaft für Technische Zusam-menarbeit (GTZ), a German development and sustainability organisation. Marketing of hand-pressed argan oil was undertaken by the Union of Women's Cooperatives of the Arganeraie (UCFA), which sold the oil mainly to local markets, but also to small private companies and tourist centres such as Agadir and Essaouira; and (2) mechanised cooperatives, established by Charrouf with support from the European Union (EU), Oxfam and the

Exhibit 1.20 Akkain Ouargane Women's Cooperative, established in 2007; photograph © GIZ/Tristan Vostry (with permission).

Japanese International Cooperative Agency (JICA). The aim was to speed up production, improve the quality of the oil, increase the oil's shelf-life and reduce waste.

In 2019, there were 540 women argan oil cooperatives in Morocco and 9565 members. The state's Office du Développement de la Coopération (ODCO) regulates cooperative activities and collects a 2 percent parafiscal 'cooperative development tax' on net profits (ODCO 2020). Each member pays a fee to join the cooperative and is entitled to attend the annual meetings with the right to vote. The members should receive a standardised wage, based on their output, and shares of the annual profits. They are provided with literacy classes, health services, childcare and opportunities to travel to different events. Six members in each argan oil cooperative are elected to leadership roles, which include the president, vice-president, secretary and treasurer. In addition, each cooperative employs staff to operate the machinery (Exhibit 1.17), an employee to sell products in the retail store (Exhibits 1.21 and 1.22), and a director (Exhibit 1.23) to manage the cooperative. Most of the argan oil cooperatives belong to an association, ranging in size from 5 to 22 cooperatives, which promote the cooperative movement and are affiliated to the national association, 'Association Nationale des Coopératives Arganières'.

Exhibit 1.21 Argan oil products being sold at the retail store of the Tighanimine Women's Cooperative; photograph © Suzanne Jones, https://thetravelbunny.com/ (with permission).

Exhibit 1.22 Bottle of pure argan oil purchased at a cooperative retail store; photograph © A. Allan Degen

Exhibit 1.23 Jamila Raissi, managing director of the Akkain Ouargane Women's Cooperative, checking the argan oil produced; photograph © GIZ/Tristan Vostry (with permission).

Strides have been made to protect the argan oil enterprise in Morocco. Adulteration can be detected which ascertains argan oil purity of up to 98% (Hilali et al., 2007). Currently, there are two cooperatives with Fairtrade certification. Fairtrade means that the women receive a fair salary that allows them to afford life's essentials, such as food, education and healthcare. Fairtrade also certifies good working conditions, capacity building and no discrimination, child labour or forced labour. With these criteria, job security is improved and poverty is reduced. In 2011, Tighanimine, established near Agadir in 2007, was the first argan oil cooperative to be granted Fairtrade certification (Exhibit 1.24). To achieve this recognition, assistance was provided from the Ibn Al Baytar association and the Belgian Trade for Development Centre (Skog, 2013). Nadia Fatmi, who gave literacy classes at the cooperative, became the cooperative director and then was elected as the chairperson of the Fairtrade North African Board. This cooperative also received an award by the Moroccan Network for Social and Solidarity Economy and the Pan-African Institute for Development for its work in good governance and economic development (Fairtrade, 2013). In 2017, the Ajdig N'Targuinine Women's Cooperative, established in 2005 in Agadir,

Exhibit 1.24 Tighanimine, established in 2007, was the first argan oil cooperative to be granted Fairtrade certification in 2011; photograph © Suzanne Jones, https://thetravelbunny.com/ (with permission).

also received certification. Argan oil was registered as a protected geographical indication (PGI) under Moroccan law in 2010 — the first product in Africa to receive such recognition. Charrouf, with the help of the Ministry of Agriculture, the Aquitaine region (France) and OriGIn (Organisation for an International Geographical Indications Network), facilitated the process. A PGI ensures that argan oil and its production meets specific standards and is a genuine Moroccan product. These standards make it easy to detect unofficial and fake argan-based products, thus protecting local producers and consumers (WIPO, undated). The Moroccan government applied for a PGI for argan oil with the EU in 2011.

le Polain de Waroux and Lambin (2013) classified argan oil as a biological resource-based niche commodity (BNC), as it is derived from an edemic species of restricted distribution and is a specialty item sold in small quantities at high prices. These authors presented five reasons for a strong global market and high prices for argan oil: '(1) part of the production is certified organic, and the rising market value of oil is thought to encourage ecosystem conservation by producers; (2) it is associated with a gender empowerment and rural development narrative; (3) it has desirable health properties both as cosmetic and edible oil; (4) it is used as a gourmet seasoning in high-end Western restaurants; and (5) it is associated with an "Edenic" narrative (Bryant and Goodman, 2004) emphasising Berber identity and tradition'.

Argan oil became the most expensive oil in the world, selling for $300 to $400 a litre. In 2019, the global argan oil market reached $223.9 million, and, with a compound annual growth rate of 10.8%, is predicted to reach $507.2 million in 2027. The oil and its products are sold to the United States, Canada, Mexico, Germany, United Kingdom, France, China, India, Japan, Brazil, Morocco and Gulf Cooperation Council. North Americans were the largest consumers in 2019 at 35.4% of the market, which was attributed to their preference for bio-based personal care, cosmetics, and aromatherapy products. Business-to-business sales by internet, wholesalers and value-added distributors accounts for approximately 60% of the sales; whereas business to consumer sales through stores, online outlets and door-to-door accounts for approximately 40%. Much of the oil is distributed globally by Moroccan agents such as OLVEA, ARGANisme, Zineglob, Purus International, Malakbio, Argane Aouzac, Organica Group LTD, Arganfarm, Zidrop Argan Oil and Arganbulk, while foreign cosmetic firms, such as L'Oréal/Garnier, BASF, Unilever and Oriflame, incorporate argan oil in their products (Grand View Research, 2020; Perry, 2020). These firms usually sign agreements with cooperatives to purchase their oil and, generally, to support the cooperatives. Some associations, including Targanine and Tizargane, that represent several cooperatives distribute products such as Arganati, a cooking oil, Arganium, a cosmetic oil and Amlou Beldi, a spread (Charrouf and Guillaume, 2009).

Impact of Argan Oil on Amazigh Women

Has the argan oil boom benefitted the Amazigh women who introduced the oil to the world? According to Robinson (2020) in his book, 'The Moroccan Argan Trade: Producer Networks and Human Bio-Geographies', the cooperatives and businesses were encroached partially or entirely by men as the value of the oil increased, even though cooperatives marketed the oil as 'women empowerment'. The Belgian Development Agency, BEFAIR, estimated that less than 10% of the argan oil exported from Morocco is produced by authentic women's cooperatives. Instead, the oil is produced by fake cooperatives, known as 'ghost cooperatives', which are controlled by local business people whose employees are paid far below fair labor rates (Healy, 2016).

Lybbert et al. (2010) reported that women who collected more kernels in 1999 had more goats in 2007, and more of their girls were enrolled in school. But it had no effect on boy's enrollment. In addition, the presence of a cooperative in the vicinity did not affect the flock size of goats. Large differences were reported in earnings by the women. Many of the women in the cooperatives complained about low salaries but explained that they had little choice of employment (Rosengren, 2020). In a WIPO (undated) report, in 2010, women in the cooperatives were earning 6 Euros per day, which was about 10 times the amount they were earning on their own. Rosengren (2020) reported that women in cooperatives earn approximately $221 a month, which is below the minimal wage, and, although most women work long hours, some earn as little as $50 a month. The median income at the cooperatives, according to Perry (2020), was $1.71 per day, ranging between $0.11 and $7.27, and $119 per month, ranging between $2.57 and $174.42, all well below the minimal wage. Women were paid according to their production but, as many were innumerate, could not calculate how much they should be paid. In addition, payments were often irregular in some cooperatives and the women had to wait weeks before receiving their salaries. The contribution of earnings from argan oil to the total overall household budget averaged only 4.1%, which was less than the contributions of argan wood and agriculture, and played a minor role in the budget and asset accumulation. Remittances by the husband accounted for 35%, the largest contribution to the budget (le Polain de Waroux and Lambin, 2013).

Apparently, there are large differences among the cooperatives in how women are treated and how their status is affected (Dupraz-Dobias, 2016). Some women expressed they gained self-esteem and confidence in their ability and that employment at the argan oil cooperative enhanced their social role in the community and their respect from peers. They also experienced greater camaraderie and solidarity with other women (le Polain de Waroux, 2013). The money they earned allowed them to accumulate more assets, pay school tuition for their children and buy clothes. In contrast, Perry (2020) reported that, although the women's workload increased substantially when employed by the cooperative, there was no increase in their status, they felt less respect from family members and lower solidarity with women of the community, and they had less mobility outside the community unaccompanied by a man. In addition, literacy did not improve among cooperative workers and might have even decreased slightly, in spite of the literacy classes. However, Perry (2020) did report that women in the cooperative were more likely to feel more optimistic about improving their lives, to earn and save money and to vote. Perhaps, data from Perry's (2020) survey could explain, at least in part, the contrasting responses by the women. The findings revealed that one-third of the cooperatives were directed by educated, able businesswomen; whereas, two-thirds were directed by inept personnel who were accused of mismanagement, exploitation, corruption, and fraud.

Argan oil production has undergone many changes over the years. Traditionally, only Amazigh women produced the oil, and the whole process was done manually. Today, much of the process is mechanised and approximately 95% of the women just crack nuts. Control of argan oil production shifted from Amazigh women to the Moroccan state and businessmen and 99% of the argan forests is owned publically.

Acknowledgements

I am grateful to Nadav Solowey (Kibbutz Ketura, Israel), Wendy Perry (Boyd Caton Group, Inc., Charlottesville, VA, USA), Emily de Riel (Fairtrade International), Yann le Polain de Waroux (McGill University, Montreal, QC, Canada) and Sheila Warshawsky (Omer, Israel) for helpful information on argan oil and Amazigh women, and Felix Grohe (Deutsche Gesellschaft für Internationale Zusammenarbeit (GIZ) GmbH), Valérie Heuzé (Feedipedia) and Suzanne Jones (Travelbunny) for permission to use photographs.

References

ADD (Africa's Development Dynamics) (2018), "Growth, Jobs and Inequalities," https://doi.org/10.1787/9789264302501-enAUC/OECD

Agence France-Presse, 2020IMF (2020), "Berbers: North Africa's Marginalized Indigenous People," https://www.courthousenews.com/berbers-north-africas-marginalized-indigenous-people/

Aithammou, R., C. Harrouni, L. Aboudlou, A. Hallouti, M. Mlouk, A. Elasbahani, and S. Daou (2019), "Effect of Clones, Year of Harvest and Geographical Origin of Fruits on Quality and Chemical Composition of Argan Oil," *Food Chemistry* 297, p. 124749.

Alados, C. L., and A. El Aich (2008), "Stress Assessment of Argan (*Argania spinosa* (L.) Skeels) in Response to Land Uses Across an Aridity Gradient: Translational Asymmetry and Branch Fractal Dimension," *Journal of Arid Environments* 72, pp. 338–349.

Argan Oil Direct (undated), "The Argan Oil Co-Operatives," https://argan oildirect.com/argan-oil-production-and-women-co-operatives

Barnett, S. (2020), "After Mass Exodus, Morocco Celebrates its Jewish heritage," *The Jewish News of Northern California,* https://jweekly.com/2020/03/06/shifting-sands-after-mass-exodus-jewish-morocco-blooms-again/

Batta, F. Z., T. S. Houssaini, K. Alaoui Sekkouri, H. Alaoui, S. Dahri, K. Alaoui Belghiti, M. Arrayhani, M. Errasfa, S. Mohamed, B. Abdellah, and M. Fez (2016), "Hemodialysis Associated Dyslipidemia: Effect of Virgin Argan Oil Consumption," *Journal of International Research in Medical and Pharmaceutical Sciences* 9, pp. 139–145.

Belahsen, B., K. Naciri|, and A. El Ibrahimi (2017), "Food Security and Women's Roles in Moroccan Berber (Amazigh) Society Today," *Maternal and Child Nutrition* 13 (S3), p. e12562.

Bordat, S. W., S. S. Davis, and S. Kouzzi (2011), "Women as Agents of Grassroots Change: Illustrating Micro-Empowerment in Morocco," *Journal of Middle East Women's Studies* 7 (1), pp. 90–119.

Bryant, R. L., and M. K Goodman (2004), "Consuming Narratives: The Political Ecology of "Alternative" Consumption", *Transactions of the Institute of British Geographers* 29 (3), pp. 344–366.

Cabrera-Vique, C., R. Marfil, R. Giménez, and O. Martínez-Augustin (2012), "Bioactive Compounds and Nutritional Significance of Virgin Argan Oil — an Edible Oil with Potential as a Functional Food," *Nutrition Reviews* 70 (5), pp. 266–279.

Cayuela, J. A., M. Rada, M. Pérez-Camino, B. Benaissa, E. Addelaziz, and A. Guinda (2008), "Characterization of Artisanally and Semi-Automatically Extracted Argan Oils from Morocco," *European Journal of Lipid Science and Technology* 110 (12), pp. 1159–1166.

Charrad, M. M. (2012), "Family Law Reforms in the Arab World: Tunisia and Morocco," Report for the United Nations department of Economic and Social Affairs (UNDESA).

Charrouf, Z., and D. Guillaume (2008), "Argan Oil, Functional Food, and the Sustainable Development of the Argan Forest," *Natural Product Communications* 3 (2), pp. 283–288.

Charrouf, Z., and D. Guillaume (2009), "Sustainable Development in Northern Africa: The Argan Forest Case," *Sustainability* 1, pp. 1012–1022.

Charrouf, Z., and D. Guillaume (2018), "The Argan Oil Project: Going from Utopia to Reality in 20 Years," *Ocl - Oleagineux Corps Gras Lipides,* 25 (2), D209, https://doi.org/10.1051/ocl/2018006

Charrouf, Z., H. Harhar, S. Gharby, and S. Guillaume (2008), "Enhancing the Value of Argan Oil is the Best Mean to Sustain the Argan Grove Economy and Biodiversity, so Far," *Ocl - Oleagineux Corps Gras Lipides* 15 (4), pp. 269–271.

Charrouf, Z., S. Dubé, and D. Guillaume (2011), *L'arganier et l'huile d'argane, d'Ibn Al-Baytar à nos jours,* Paris, France: Ed Glyphe.

Dana, L. P. (2006), "Business Values Among the Imazighen," *Euromed Journal of Business* 1 (2), pp. 82–89.

Dana, L. P., and T. E. Dana (2008), "Ethnicity and Entrepreneurship in Morocco: A Photo-Ethnographic study," *International Journal of Business and Globalization* 2 (3), pp. 209–226.

Dossa, Z. (2011), "Cooperatives: A Development Strategy? An Analysis of Argan Oil Cooperatives in Southwest Morocco," Euricse Working Paper, N.029 | 12.

Dupraz-Dobias, P. (2016), "How Berber Women are Fighting Desertification," https://www.swissinfo.ch/eng/marrakech-effect_how-berber-women-are-fighting-desertification/42591500

El Aissati, A. (2005), "A Socio-Historical Perspective on the Amazigh (Berber) Cultural Movement in North Africa," *Afrika Focus* 18 (1–2), pp. 59–72.

Essouiri, J., T. Harzy, N. Benaicha, M. Errasfa, and F. Ee Abourazzak (2017), "Effectiveness of Argan Oil on Knee Osteoarthritis Symptoms: A Randomized Controlled Clinical Trial," *Current Rheumatology Reviews* 13 (3), pp. 231–235.

Fairtrade (2013), "Fairtrade on the Road," https://fairtrade.tumblr.com/post/45105818691/the-women-of-the-tighanimine-cooperative-the

Gharby, S., H. Harhar, B. Kartah, D. Guillaume, I. Chafchaouni-Moussaoui, and Z. Charrouf (2014), "Oxidative Stability of Cosmetic Argan Oil: A One-Year Study," *Journal of Cosmetic Science* 65 (2), pp. 81–88.

Gharby, S., H. Harhar, D. Guillaume, A. Haddad, B. Matthäus, and Z. Charrouf (2011), "Oxidative Stability of Edible Argan Oil: A Two-Year Period Study," *LWT-Food Science and Technology* 44, pp. 1–8.

Grand View Research (2020), *Argan Oil Market Size, Share and Trends Analysis Report,* Grand View Research, San Francisco, CA, USA, https://www.grandviewresearch.com/industry-analysis/argan-oil-market.

Guillaume, D., and Z. Charrouf (2011), "Argan Oil," *Alternative Medicine Review* 16 (3), pp. 275–279.

HDR (Human Development Report) (2020), "The Next Frontier: Human Development and the Anthropocene, United Nations Development Programme," http://hdr.undp.org/sites/default/files/hdr2020.pdf

Healy, E. (2016), "Evan's Journey to the Al Amal Women's Co-Operative," https://www.evanhealy.com/blogs/stories/al-amal-womens-co-operative-journey

Hilali, M., Z. Charrouf, A. El Azziz Soulhi, L. Hachimi, and D. Guillaume (2007), "Detection of Argan Oil Adulteration Using Campesterol GC-Analysis," *Journal of the American Oil Chemists' Society* 84, pp. 761–764.

Hoffman, K. E. (2008), *We Share Walls: Language, Land, and Gender in Berber Morocco*, Malden, MA: Wiley-Blackwell.

Huang, P. (2017), "Liquid Gold: Berber Women and the Argan Oil Co-Operatives in Morocco," *International Journal of Intangible Heritage* 12, pp. 140–155.

Ilhiane, I. (1999), "The Berber Agdal Institution: Indigenous Range Management in the Atlas Mountains," *Ethnology* 38 (1), pp. 21–45.

IMF (International Monetary Fund) (2020), "World Economic Databases," https://www.imf.org/en/Publicatios/SPROLLs/world-economic-outlook-databases#sort=%40imfdate%20descending

Kenny, L., and I. DeZborowski (2007), "Biologie de l'arganier," in *Atlas de l'arganier et de l'arganeraie*, Rabat, Morocco: Hassan II IAV.

Kisaalita, W., M. Shealy, M. J. Neu, P. Jones, and J. Dunn (2010), "Argan Nut Cracker for Southwestern Moroccan Women," *Agricultural Mechanization in Asia, Africa and Latin America* 41 (1), pp. 27–33.

Knoema (2020), "World Data Atlas – Morocco – Demographics," https://knoema.com/atlas/Morocco/Population

le Polain de Waroux, Y. (2013), "The Social and Environmental Context of Argan Oil Production," *Natural Product Communications* 8 (1), pp. 1–4.

le Polain de Waroux, Y., and E. F. Lambin (2011), "Monitoring Degradation in Arid and Semi-Arid Forests and Woodlands: The Case of the Argan Woodlands (Morocco)," *Applied Geography* 32, pp. 777–786.

le Polain de Waroux, Y., and E. F. Lambin (2013), "Niche Commodities and Rural Poverty Alleviation: Contextualizing the Contribution of Argan Oil to Rural Livelihoods in Morocco," *Annals of the Association of American Geographers* 103 (3), pp. 589–607.

Lybbert, T. J. (2007), "Patent Disclosure Requirements and Benefit Sharing: A Counterfactual Case of Morocco's Argan Oil," *Ecological Economics* 64 (1), pp. 12–18.

Lybbert, T. J., A. Aboudrare, D. Chaloud, N. Magnan, and M. Nash (2011), "Booming Markets for Moroccan Argan Oil Appear to Benefit Some Rural Households while Threatening the Endemic Argan Forest," *Proceedings of the National Academy of Sciences* 108 (34), pp. 13963–13968.

Lybbert, T. J., N. Magnan, and A. Aboudrare (2010), "Household and Local Forest Impacts of Morocco's Argan Oil Bonanza," *Environment and Development Economics* 15 (4), pp. 439–464.

Maddy-Weitzman, B. (2006), "Ethno-Politics and Globalisation in North Africa: The Berber Culture Movement," *The Journal of North African Studies* 11 (1), pp. 71–83.

Mounir, F., M. Jourrane, and M. Sabir (2015), "Analyse basée télédétection pour la révision de la carte de répartition des peuplements a arganeraie et comparaison diachronique de sa dynamique spatiotemporelle," Actes du 3e congrès International de l'Arganier, 2011, Agadir, Morrocco, p. 36.

MSN Encarta (2009), "Morocco, Microsoft and Encarta - Online Encyclopedia," http://encarta.msn.com

New World Encyclopedia (2019), "Berber," https://www.newworldencyclopedia.org/p/index.php?title=Berber&oldid=1027593>

Norme SNIMA (2003), "Service de normalisation industrielle marocaine (Snima)," Corps gras d'origine animale ou végétale huiles d'argan, Spécification Norme Marocaine, NM 08.5.090, Rabat.

ODCO (Office du Développement de la Coopération) (2020), "Morocco," https://coops4dev.coop/en/4devafrica/morocco

Peabody Museum (2021), *Imazighen! Beauty and artisanship in Berber life*, Peabody Museum of Archaeology and Ethnology, Harvard University, Cambridge, MA.

Perry, W. (2020), "Social Sustainability and the Argan Boom as Green Development in Morocco," *World Development Perspectives* 20, p. 100238.

Perry, W., O. Rappe, A. Boulhaoua, L. H. Loux, Y. Elhouss, H. A. Ahssain, Z. A. Barich, H. Akhiyat, T. A. Aznague, and S. Hraïd (2019), "Argan Oil and the Question of Empowerment in Rural Morocco," *The Journal of North African Studies* 24 (5), pp. 830–859.

Robinson, D. F. (2020). *The Moroccan Argan Trade: Producer Networks and Human Bio-Geographies,* Avon, United Kingdom: Routledge.

Rosengren, I. (2020), "The Women who Make Argan Oil Want Better Pay," https://www.bbc.com/news/business-51370010

Ruas, M. P., J. Ros, J-F. Terral, S. Ivorra, H. Andrianarinosy, A. S. Ettahiri, A. Fili, and J-P. V. Staëvel (2015), "History and Archaeology of the Emblematic Argan Tree in the Medieval Anti-Atlas Mountains (Morocco)," *Quaternary International* 404, pp. 114–136.

Schwartz, Y. (2019), "Moroccan Vilagers with a Hazy Jewish Tie Get a Financial Lifeline from Israelis," *The Times of Israel,* https://www.timesofisrael.com/impoverished-moroccan-villagers-get-financial-lifeline-from-israeli-crowdfunding/

Skog, B. S. (2013), *Tree of Empowerment: Women's Argan Oil Cooperatives in Morocco,* MSc dissertation, Utrecht University, Netherlands, .

Tampa Bay Times (2016), "All Eyes Photograph Gallery: The Amazigh have Lived for Millennia in Morocco's Atlas Mountains," https://www.tampabay.com/features/travel/all-eyes-photograph-gallery-the-amazigh-have-lived-for-millennia-in-moroccos/2267797/

Turner, B. (2016), "Supply-Chain Legal Pluralism: Normativity as Constitutive of Chain Infrastructure in the Moroccan Argan Oil Supply Chain," *The Journal of Legal Pluralism and Unofficial Law* 48 (3), pp. 78–414.

UNDP (United Nations Development Programme) (2018), "Human Development Data (1990–2017)," http://hdr.undp.org/en/data

UNESCO (2002), "Biosphere Reserve Information: Morocco, Arganeraie," http://www.unesco.org/mabdb/br/brdir/directory/biores.asp?code=MOR+01&mode=all

WIPO (World Intellectual Property Organization) (undated), "Protecting Society and the Environment with a Geographical Indication," https://www.wipo.int/ipadvantage/en/articles/article_0111.html

© 2022 World Scientific Publishing Company
https://doi.org/10.1142/9789811236600_0002

Chapter 2

Women Entrepreneurs in Morocco

Lyn S. Amine
Saint Louis University, USA

Abstract

This study explores the lived experience of women entrepreneurs (WEs), addressing the question 'What is it like to be a self-employed woman in Morocco?' An international marketing analysis of Morocco and real-life vignettes of WEs complement a SWOT analysis of what the future holds for Moroccan WEs. Recommendations include a national marketing campaign to inform current and potential WEs of available resources, facilitate uptake, build community and transform inefficient national business practices that undermine each woman's best efforts. Improved articulation of Morocco's business ecosystem will benefit WEs immeasurably.

Keywords: women entrepreneurs, self-employed women, Morocco, national marketing campaign, ecosystem

Introduction

Morocco is a land that evokes rich imagery (Exhibit 2.1) from the mysterious (Exhibit 2.2) to the exotic (Exhibit 2.3) to the magical to the modern and exciting, conveyed in films such as *Casablanca, The Road to Morocco, Babel, The Sheltering Sky* and *The Bourne Ultimatum. Game of Thrones* was filmed in three towns: Ouarzazate (Exhibit 2.4) in the desert southeast, the coastal kite-surfing resort of Essaouira, and the royal capital, Rabat. The 1985 motion picture *The Jewel of the Nile* was filmed in part at Ait Benhaddou (Exhibit 2.5).

Exhibit 2.1 Rich imagery in Morocco; photograph © Léo-Paul Dana

Exhibit 2.2 Berber pharmacy; photograph © Léo-Paul Dana

Exhibit 2.3 Shop in Marrakesh; photograph © Léo-Paul Dana

Exhibit 2.4 Ouarzazate; photograph © Léo-Paul Dana

Exhibit 2.5 Ait Benhaddou; photograph © Léo-Paul Dana

Morocco's diverse range of topography, landscapes, climate, villages (Exhibit 2.6) and cities (Exhibit 2.7) provides many choices for film directors and tourists, ranging from snow-capped mountains to ancient desert forts to coastal towns and traditional kasbahs. The country's abundant natural and human resources position it as the world's leading producer of phosphates, a land of bountiful agriculture (Exhibit 2.8), an efficient manufacturing base and a favourite tourist destination (Exhibit 2.9).

This paper explores the lived experience of women entrepreneurs (WEs) in Morocco from a business point of view, addressing the question 'What is it like to be a self-employed woman in Morocco?' The term 'woman entrepreneur' describes women who start their own business either alone, with or without employees, or as a member of a group providing mutual support such as a cooperative.

Women's entrepreneurship has been investigated using frameworks such as institutional theory (Amine and Staub, 2008), feminism, agency theory, race theory, public policy and psychology to name but a few. Some studies serve an explanatory purpose by identifying push/pull factors motivating entrepreneurs as well as causes and effects driving the performance of WEs. Others adopt a comparative approach such as the Gender-GEDI study (Aidis et al., 2013) of conditions for entrepreneurship across seventeen countries including Morocco. Others take a public policy perspective, examining government-sponsored educational programmes and training schemes designed to prepare women for business as entrepreneurs. This study adopts an international marketing approach consistent with a broader ecosystem perspective embracing interacting elements fostering new firm creation in a specific context (Neck et al., 2004).

Exhibit 2.6 Village in the Atlas mountains; photograph © Léo-Paul Dana

Exhibit 2.7 Place Djema el Fna, Marrakesh; photograph © Léo-Paul Dana

Exhibit 2.8 Farm; photograph © Léo-Paul Dana

Exhibit 2.9 Orange juice market popular with tourists; photograph © Léo-Paul Dana

The chapter is organised in four sections. The Introduction presents Morocco as a sovereign, forward-looking and cosmopolitan nation. The Historical Overview identifies geographical, historical, political, economic, cultural and linguistic factors that have shaped the nation's sense of identity and position in the world. Women and Entrepreneurship presents real-life vignettes of WEs in Morocco and Toward the Future assesses how current trends will affect WEs in Morocco.

Five theoretical frameworks provide structure. In the Historical Overview, Cateora et al.'s (2020) environmental model, originally developed for international marketing managers planning entry into a new country, illustrates the range of contextual knowledge that is indispensable to understand how business operates in any socio-economic or political environment, whether foreign or domestic. Hofstede-Insights (2021) cultural analysis of Morocco identifies values shaping attitudes and behaviours in the Moroccan marketplace. In *Women and Entrepreneurship*, Brush et al.'s (2010) Gender-Embeddedness 5M framework identifies five components of women's experience of entrepreneurship and Aidis et al.'s (2013) Gender-GEDI framework analyses 15 'pillars' of entrepreneurship. In *Toward the Future*, a SWOT analysis addresses strengths and weaknesses, opportunities and threats driving the future of WEs in Morocco.

In 2020, an international political event occurred that had profound impact on Morocco as a sovereign nation. Under the 'Abraham Accords', former President Trump formally recognised Moroccan sovereignty over the Western Sahara, effectively increasing Morocco's land mass by about 60%,as part of an agreement that Morocco would normalise relations with Israel. This intervention by the US president addressed a decades-long dispute with Spain, Algeria, Mauritania and the Polisario guerrilla resistance group over status of the Western Sahara, located at the southern tip of Morocco (see Lovatt and Mundy, 2021 for a full discussion). Official Moroccan government maps and those used by NATO, the US Department of State and the CIA no longer show any border demarcating the Western Sahara as a separate political entity.

This region, known as the 'southern province', is critically important to Morocco's political and economic future. Territorial waters in the Atlantic Ocean have rich fishing areas and underwater mineral resources while the region's airspace has strategic value to Morocco and its allies, not least as a former transoceanic abort landing (TAL) site for NASA. The region offers extensive solar and wind energy resources along with phosphates, iron ore, copper, uranium, and oil and natural gas deposits onshore and offshore awaiting exploitation. Morocco imports 91% of its gas and 99% of its oil requirements so energy diversification and self-sufficiency have long been critical goals. The launch in 2009 of the NOOR solar energy project was a commitment to sustainability, with the goal of reaching 52% renewable energy in the power mix by 2030 (Renewables Now, 2021).

With an estimated population of some 611,000 Sahrawis (Worldometer, 2021), the former Western Sahara is one of the most sparsely populated areas of the world. Since the Abraham Accords, there have been rapid inflows of enormous foreign direct investment (FDI) by EU countries, the United States, Russia and China especially in the mining and energy sectors and many nations have announced their intention to build consulates in the province.

Morocco is a constitutional monarchy dating back to the 17th century. The current monarch, King Mohamed VI, completed his PhD in law at the French University of Nice Sophia Antipolis with a thesis on 'EEC-Maghreb Relations.' The King has demonstrated a modern mindset, marrying a career businesswoman and explicitly championing women's rights and equality through new legal protections. A prime minister heads both the executive and legislative branches of government and the elected Parliament features a quota system for female representation which reached 21% in 2016 (North Africa Post, 2016).

In the 20th century, Morocco was a French protectorate under a contract initiated in 1912 and peacefully terminated in 1956. The legacy of French culture and language is integral to understanding Morocco as a bilingual, bicultural nation where 'code-switching' between Moroccan Arabic (Darija) and French routinely occurs in conversation. In northern Morocco and the former Western Sahara, Spanish is spoken alongside Darija and French, a legacy of former Spanish colonial influence.

Many young people and users of social media are also comfortable in English, if not proficient. In 2004, the Free Trade Agreement between Morocco and the United States underlined the importance of English in international business. It also cemented Morocco's longstanding relationship with the United States, dating back to 1777 when Morocco was the first nation to recognise America's independence (US-Morocco Free Trade Agreement, 2021). Under the Abraham Accords, trade relations are likely to shift as the US plans $3 billion in new investments in Morocco (Haaretz, 2020). However, according to Hatim (2021a), lack of national proficiency and marketing in English is hindering inward other FDI due to traditional reliance on trade with France and Spain.

The population of Morocco was 37 million in 2021, slightly less than the population of California (39 million), which is similar in physical size. Population growth is slowed somewhat by negative net annual migration of about 50,000 Moroccans going abroad to work and study. The Moroccan diaspora numbers 5–6 million and remittances are a critical component of the economy, reaching $7.05 billion in 2020 (Kasraoui, 2021; Morocco Population, 2021).

Generations of Moroccan men living abroad have married foreign wives, introducing an element of cosmopolitanism into their family of origin in Morocco. Most families have at least one member living outside the country, either working or studying, especially in France, Spain, Italy, Francophone Canada and the United Arab Emirates. Family gatherings during annual visits home or virtual get-togethers resemble a United Nations of languages and identities of multi-generational families born outside Morocco. This rich cultural mix affects families at all levels of income, resulting in an outward-looking population. In 2021, the government launched a digital platform *Bladifqalbi* (literally: my country in my heart) to strengthen ties with the Moroccan diaspora, providing a platform for video commentary and access to public services such as passport renewal and payment of taxes (https://bladifqalbi.ma/).

Historical Overview

Elements of Cateora et al.'s (2020) model (Exhibit 2.10) are discussed under three headings:

- Influence of History and Geography on Morocco's Trade Relations
- Political and Cultural Influences in the Marketplace
- Cultural Values in the Entrepreneurial Ecosystem

Influence of History and Geography on Morocco's Trade Relations

Morocco's history is a product of its unique strategic location on the northwestern tip of the African continent where the Atlantic Ocean meets the Mediterranean Sea. This location favours looking outward, north to Spain and Europe, east to North Africa and the Middle East, south to sub-Saharan Africa, and west to the Americas. Ancient camel caravan routes operated over centuries, supporting gold and salt trade along the north–south axis between Marrakesh and the empires of West Africa, and an east–west trade route with Libya, Egypt and Ethiopia.

In 2015, King Mohamed VI announced the new Tiznit–Dakhla highway as a flagship development project to integrate the remote southern province into the life of the nation (Hatim, 2021c). This is part of a master plan for road construction throughout the country until the year 2035, along with a north-south high-speed rail network linking coastal cities from Tangiers to Agadir, with a link to Marrakesh (Switzerland Global Enterprise, 2017).

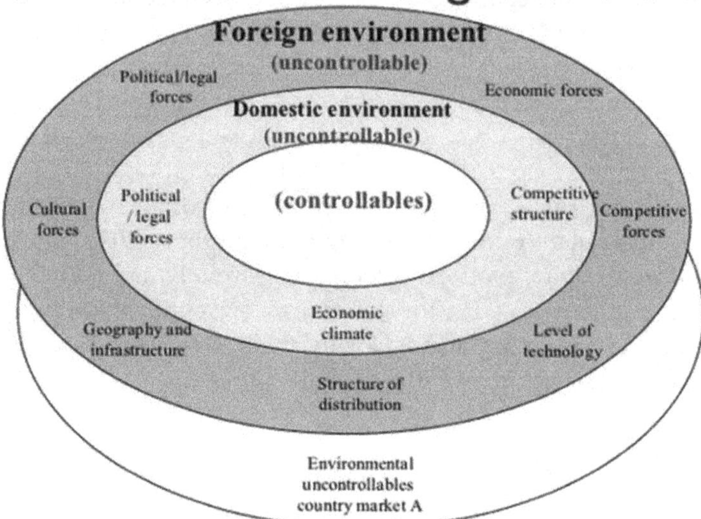

Exhibit 2.10 Factors in the international marketing environment (Cateora et al. 2020)

Fertile soil, abundant water from the Atlas Mountains and a temperate sunny climate all ensure that Morocco has a rich and varied yearlong export production of fruits, vegetables, livestock and flowers (providing essences for the French perfume market). An unexpected result of Brexit (when Britain withdrew from the EU in 2020) directly impacted Morocco's maritime trade. In 2021, a weekly shipping service for agribusiness exports was established between Poole on Britain's south coast and Tangiers. This new roll on/roll off service for containers provides a remedy for interruptions in Britain's imports of EU foodstuffs, delayed by new customs duties and documentation requirements (Fresh Fruit Portal, 2021).

The Berbers

Berber language and culture add another layer to the multi-faceted market environment of Morocco. Berbers are an ancient ethnic group who distinguish themselves from majority ethnic Arabs under the name *Amazigh*. They belong to regional clans or tribes defined by where they live, such as the Riffians in the northern Atlas, Shleuh in the Middle Atlas and Soussi in the south around Agadi. Kinship ties are reinforced through their own language Tamazight, customs and music (such as the Tuareg-Berber rock band Tinariwen). Traditional Berber arts and crafts (Exhibit 2.11) are world famous and valued by visitors to Morocco, providing self-employment opportunities to Berber women (CMES, 2021).

Traditionally, Berbers lived as farmers in rural areas (Exhibit 2.12), the Atlas Mountains and remote southern regions, whereas Berbers in urban centres specialised in retail grocery trades (see Dana, 2006). With time, their business acumen has spread throughout the Moroccan economy and government, bringing significant power and influence (Wikipedia, 2021a; Akl, 2020). The appointment of *Saad Eddine Othmani as* Head of Government (Prime Minister) by King Mohamed VI in 2017 is testament to the visibility of the Amazigh in Morocco (Igrouane, 2017). Tamazight (Exhibit 2.13) was recognised as an official language in 2011 and is used on public road-signs with modern standard Arabic and French.

The Jews

Jews still play a notable role in Morocco (see Dana and Dana, 2008). In 2021, King Mohamed VI's senior adviser was Jewish, André Azoulay and Jewish schools and synagogues receive government subsidies. At their peak, Moroccan Jews numbered well over 200,000, declining to about

Exhibit 2.11 Loom; photograph © Léo-Paul Dana

Exhibit 2.12 Rural life; photograph © Léo-Paul Dana

Exhibit 2.13 Arabic, Tamazight and French; photograph used with permission from Wikimedia

2,000 in 2019, following decades of outward migration to Israel (as well as Canada, France and the US) (Jewish Virtual Library, 2021). The State of Israel is home to nearly 1,000,000 Jews of Moroccan descent, about 15% of its total population. Around 50,000 Israelis travel to Morocco each year to visit religious sites and tourist attractions and celebrate weddings according to Moroccan tradition (Eljechtimi and Rabinovitch, 2020).

The 2020 bilateral normalisation agreement provides for direct flights between the two nations, economic cooperation, liaison offices in Rabat and Tel Aviv (to be followed by embassies) and movement towards 'full diplomatic, peaceful and friendly relations' based on a shared cultural heritage. Jewish history and culture will be taught in Moroccan schools, considered 'a first in the Arab world' by the Secretary-General of the Council of Jewish Communities of Morocco (*Arab News, 2020*). New Israeli investment targets include banking and finance, agriculture, water, environment, hotels and tourism, science and medical innovations, energy, telecommunications, aerospace technologies and cybersecurity (Dumpis, 2021b). Some 300 Israeli industrial units in the electronics field are planning operations in Morocco, creating more than 7,000 jobs and opening new possibilities for entrepreneurs (Ennaji, 2021). Exhibit 2.14 features a shop that caters to its ethnic enclave.

The Spanish

Spain and Morocco have a long and contentious history dating back to the Middle Ages. Political relations are often fraught despite a large contingent of some 770,000 Moroccan workers resident in Spain. Spain's former rule over the Western Sahara only ended in 1975 when Spain finally ceded the territory to Morocco. Currently, the status of the two Spanish city enclaves on the northern coast of Morocco, Ceuta and Melilla, remains unresolved (Bennis, 2012).

The Moors of Morocco ruled Al Andalus in southern Spain for centuries. The Almoravid and Almohad dynasties in the 11th and 12th centuries and the Nasrid dynasty (1231–1492) encouraged scholarship and culture and the three religions of Islam, Christianity and Judaism flourished under the Convivencia (co-existence). However, 1492 was a turning point in the history of Spain and Morocco. Catholic monarchs, King Ferdinand II of Aragon and Queen Isabella I of Castile seized Granada, the last Moorish stronghold in Spain, as part of the Reconquista (reconquest) and the Spanish Inquisition forced Jews and Muslims to convert to Christianity or be expelled. In 1492, between 40,000 and 100,000 Sephardic Jews sought

Exhibit 2.14 Ethnic enclave in Fez; photograph © Léo-Paul Dana

refuge in Morocco where they were welcomed under Arab traditions of hospitality. This event began four centuries of active and widespread Jewish participation in the life of Morocco, amplifying their earlier presence dating back to Roman times (Chtatou, 2019). Spanish architecture is still evident in Morocco (Exhibit 2.15).

The French

During the Protectorate, tens of thousands of French colonists took up residence in Morocco buying agricultural land, building homes and filling positions in the government and liberal professions. The coming of independence did not end French presence or influence in Morocco. For several decades after the Protectorate, young French citizens could choose to teach for two years in Morocco as a volunteer civil servant instead of completing compulsory military service in France (Ardant, 1974). As a result, many Moroccans of a certain age are still more comfortable thinking, speaking and writing in French than in Arabic, even though French is not an official national language. This deep-seated French cultural, legal, administrative and educational imprint remains part of the business environment in which Moroccan WEs must operate.

Exhibit 2.15 Opened in 1913 in Tangiers; photograph © Léo-Paul Dana

The Chinese

China does not have any colonial history in Morocco so there is little negative country-of-origin effect attached to incoming Chinese FDI. Morocco ranks second, after South Africa, as preferred destination for Chinese FDI in Africa due to its significant competitive advantages. These include country location, natural resources, manufacturing capabilities, human capital, political stability, rule of law, market size and growth.

Chinese participation in the Moroccan market is recent, diversified and is creating significant opportunities and competition for large companies and small entrepreneurs alike. Tangiers Med Port, the enormous port facility and manufacturing hub on Morocco's north coast, is receiving investment as part of China's Belt and Road Initiative (BRI). As Africa's largest port, Tangiers Med Port handled 50% of the value of all Morocco's exports in 2018 (Kasraoui, 2019b). The BRI is building global connectivity along a land-based Silk Road Economic Belt and a 21st Century Maritime Silk Road. Morocco's strategic location as gateway to Europe, Africa and North America, its free trade agreements with the EU and the United States, the availability of skilled workers and land for development make it ideal for Chinese investment as part of the 'Going Out' Policy (Wang, 2017).

Chinese interest in Morocco is not only financial. Chinese tourist arrivals grew from 10,000 in 2015 to 180,000 in 2019 increasing demand for hospitality services at major destinations like Marrakesh. Chinese presence has also grown in commercial market sectors. Since 2004, resident Chinese entrepreneurs have virtually taken over a traditional wholesale market area in multicultural Casablanca (Exhibit 2.16) creating a new Chinatown where they compete fiercely on price with local entrepreneurs (Taipei Times, 2004; Hammond, 2017).

Cultural Values in the Entrepreneurial Ecosystem

Hofstede-Insights (2021) ratings for Morocco provide insight into cultural values shaping the entrepreneurial ecosystem in which WEs operate (see Exhibit 2.17).

Power distance and individualism scores of 70 and 46, respectively, indicate that Morocco is a hierarchical and collectivistic society that attaches great value to loyalty to the family, community and other membership groups. Strong social relationships ensure that everyone takes responsibility for group members, laying the groundwork for collective

Exhibit 2.16 Hotel Transatlantique, built in 1922 in Moorish style; photograph © Léo-Paul Dana

action in industrial clusters and women's cooperatives. Moroccans' deep attachment to their family, town and region of origin is an enduring element of the national character, leading naturally to a sense of solidarity and cooperation in business. In contrast, collectivist habits suggest why some segments of the population might regard individual business activities by WEs in Morocco as unfamiliar.

The uncertainty avoidance score of 68 is associated with rigid codes of belief and behaviour, lack of tolerance for unorthodox behaviour and resistance to ideas and innovation. This explains why some WEs face hurdles when trying to launch new business activities. The very low score for long-term orientation (14) demonstrates deep respect for tradition. Security is important in individual motivation and contrasts strongly with WEs' willingness to take on risk and unknown outcomes when starting their own business.

The low score on indulgence (25) indicates a culture of social restraint. These attitudes work against WEs who are self-motivated, confident and believe that they can 'do things differently'. The low masculinity score of 53 is deemed inconclusive in Hofstede's analysis: 'The

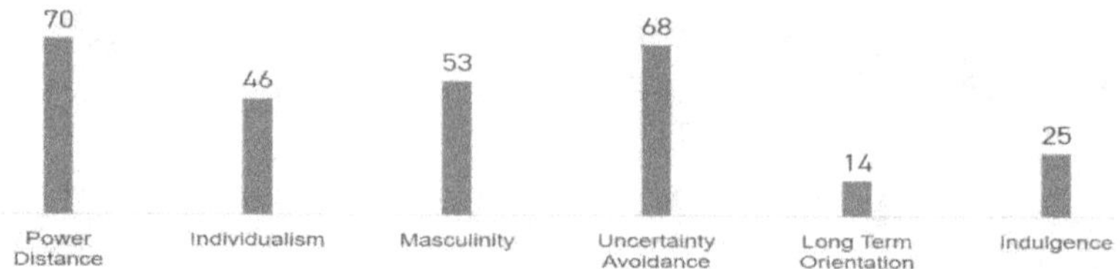

Exhibit 2.17 Hofstede's cultural analysis of Morocco (Hofstede-Insights 2021)

fundamental issue here is what motivates people, wanting to be the best (Masculine) or liking what you do (Feminine)'. Moroccan WEs demonstrate both types of motivation.

Morocco's unique combination of cultural characteristics produced a highly successful national response to the COVID-19 epidemic of 2020 and 2021, earning the accolade of 'miracle country' from the Spanish newspaper *La Razon* (Tyson, 2021) and recognition from the World Health Organisation (*North Africa Post, 2021*). Adding to Morocco's global standing was the announcement of preclinical testing in 2021 of a universal COVID-19 vaccine developed by US-Moroccan immunologist Lbachir Ben Mohamed in collaboration with the University of California-Irvine (Dumpis, 2021c).

Women and Entrepreneurship

This section addresses three topics:

- The status of women in Morocco
- Women's demographics with special attention to motherhood
- Vignettes of real-life experiences of WEs.

Status of Women in Morocco

A recurring question in any discussion of women in Muslim countries is the role of religion in shaping women's status, lifestyles and business opportunities. For some women in Morocco, life is focused on serving men (Exhibit 2.18). Yet, from a general perspective, it should be remembered that Islam allows for a married woman to own her own wealth. Mohamed married a businesswoman from a merchant family in the caravan trade, Khadija, so there is no inherent resistance to the idea of women in business in Islam. In Morocco, a Muslim woman, Fatima Al-Fihri, is honoured for founding and funding the world's oldest university, Al Qarawiyyine in Fes in the 9th century, which became a model for intellectual excellence.

A new tone was set by King Mohamed VI when he married Salma Bennani in 2001, a businesswoman aged 23 from Fes. Before marriage, Salma worked as an information services engineer at ONA Group, Morocco's industrial, financial and services conglomerate. Breaking with the tradition of strict privacy, the King's wife was given a royal title as Princess Lalla Salma and she has been widely photographed at international events such as the wedding of Britain's Prince Harry and Meghan Markle. After having two children together, the couple was rumoured to have divorced but this has never been officially confirmed. Lalla Salma is widely seen as a role model encouraging women's empowerment. She founded the Lalla Salma Foundation for Prevention and Treatment of Cancer and in 2006 was named a Goodwill Ambassador of the World Health Organisation for Cancer Care, Promotion and Prevention (Barger, 2019).

Under the King's leadership and in response to continuing political action by women's groups, the Moroccan government has made significant

Exhibit 2.18 Helping her master wash his hands; photograph © Léo-Paul Dana

efforts to remedy discrimination against women and modernise their legal status and rights. The Moroccan Family Code (Moudawana) was implemented in 2004 addressing marriage, divorce, child custody and support, legal capacity and representation, wills and the right to own and inherit property (Euromed Rights, 2012). Hallward and Stewart (2018) examined repercussions of the Moudawana in Morocco focusing on how elite background, work sector, religion and legal codes affect women's ascent to leadership roles. Results are mixed insofar as Moroccan women continue to face challenges in the social and symbolic spheres.

The persistent social problems of public harassment and domestic violence affecting the status and daily lives of Moroccan women were addressed by new legislation in 2013. The Hakkaoui Law finally went into effect in September 2018 outlawing cyber and in-person public sexual harassment, sexual exploitation and forced marriage with minors, imposing fines and terms of imprisonment. Yet changes in attitudes and behaviours are not guaranteed by laws and in 2019 effective implementation mechanisms for reporting, investigation and prosecution were still not in place (Kasraoui, 2019a).

In 2019 the activist social media campaign #Masaktach joined the global #MeToo movement against sexual harassment and all forms of sexism (*Inside Arabia, 2019*). In Morocco the concept of empowerment has only recently been translated as *tamkine* and is understood somewhat surprisingly in the context of one of the UN's SDGs addressing violence against women. The Tamkine programme unites 13 national agencies and 50 NGOs (non-governmental organisations) to fight gender-based violence (SDGF, 2021). This is the world in which WEs must operate.

Women's Demographics with Special Attention to Motherhood

Five factors affecting women's experience of entrepreneurship in Brush et al.'s (2010) 5M model are market, money, management, motherhood and the meso/macro environments (see Exhibit 2.19). Of particular interest here are the last three: motherhood represents the household/family context in which WEs operate; the meso environment reflects intermediate structures and institutions; and the macro environment refers to expectations of society and cultural norms, consistent with Cateora et al.'s (2020) environmental model.

Bouzekraoui and Ferhane (2017) and Asli and Habiba Bensassi (2018) present empirical data on WEs' demographics in Morocco offering insights into the complex cultural and socio-economic experience of women who choose to become self-employed. In order to understand the qualitative experience of WEs

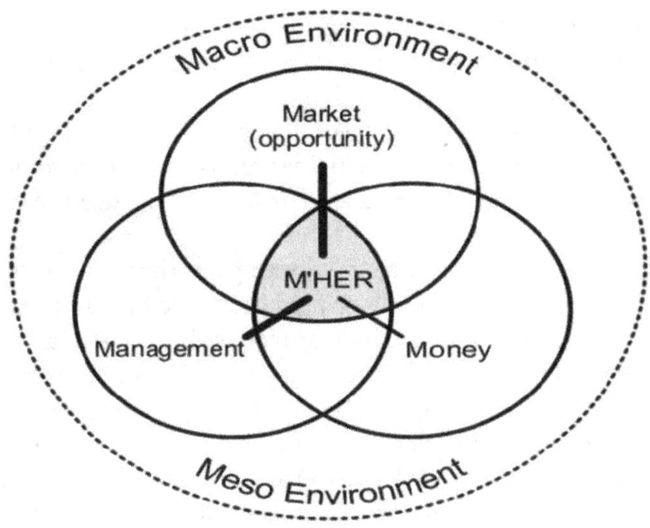

Exhibit 2.19 Gender-embeddedness 5M model of entrepreneurship, Source: (Brush et al. 2010)

in Morocco, attention is focused here on (i) population and age distribution, (ii) employment and motherhood and (iii) wealth, social class and networks.

(i)   Population and Age Distribution
In 2020, 63.5% of the population lived in urban areas along the Atlantic and Mediterranean coasts. In 2021, the population of Casablanca, the major port and commercial centre was 3.8 million (comparable to Cape Town). The capital Rabat had 1.9 million inhabitants, the ancient capital city Fes 1.25 million, the northern port and manufacturing hub Tangiers 1.24 million and the two southern resort towns Marrakesh and Agadir had populations of 1.02 million and 942,000 respectively (CIA World Factbook, 2021). Morocco is a young country with a median age of 29 years. The estimated birth rate for women in Morocco is 2.29 children, down from five in the 1980s due to higher contraceptive use, delayed marriage and the desire for smaller families (World Bank Group, 2021).

(ii)   Employment and Motherhood
Persistently poor-quality public schooling in Morocco results in a high number of dropouts, inadequate preparation for work and a disproportionately

negative impact on girls, perpetuating social disparities and limiting social mobility (Koundouno, 2019). Young women make up 76% of NEETs (not in education, employment or training) of which 36% come from rural backgrounds and almost 55% are rural housewives with family responsibilities. Women's labour force participation as a percentage of the population over 15 years old has fluctuated around 25% since the early 1990s (Dumpis, 2021a).

Moroccan WEs' experience as working mothers is constrained by the availability of extended family or paid domestic help to provide childcare. A traditional feature of life in Morocco is the cascading hierarchy of domestic employment where households at each level of income employ help from the level below until the limits of practicality are reached. Domestic employees (Exhibit 2.20) are routinely responsible for babies and children until they reach school age. In rural areas, collective bargaining is beginning to improve women's working conditions, resulting in collective solutions to childcare problems (Ford Foundation, 2019).

(iii) Wealth, Social Class and Networks

Wealth in Morocco is unevenly distributed, and lifestyles of the social classes are sharply and visibly different. Despite socio-political reforms, the country is still marked by 'alarming social inequalities' and an increasing income inequality gap. Job insecurity and inadequate wages are primary concerns with 60% of all Moroccans working in the informal sector

Exhibit 2.20 Employees; photograph © Léo-Paul Dana

(Koundouno, 2018). According to the Association of Women Entrepreneurs of Morocco (AFEM) President, Asmaa Morine Azzouzi, a primary challenge to decrease the rich-poor gap is to promote gender equality by 'boosting female entrepreneurship, investing in innovative start-ups and ensuring linkages between formal training and labour market's demands'. However, in 2015 WEs were still only 10% of all entrepreneurs in Morocco (ID4D, 2016).

Six social classes can be broadly identified in Morocco. At the top of the socio-economic hierarchy is the royal family, the Palace and influential members of the government who are also big business owners or have holdings that make them very wealthy, the 'movers and shakers' of Moroccan society. Next is the upper-middle class of professional university-educated men and women, many of whom have had experience of living, working or studying outside Morocco. On an equal financial, if not social, footing are businesspeople and landowners who are self-made or have inherited hard-earned family assets. Then there are lower middle-class skilled working people who rely on salary or wages from stable jobs throughout the economy. A very large working class of tradespeople, manual workers and domestic employees faces employment that is precarious or sporadic in both the formal and informal sectors. Finally, a massive sector of the population in rural areas and urban peripheries is unemployed or under-employed. Underemployment affects all sectors of the economy including both terminally qualified PhDs and unskilled workers for whom there is a lack of appropriate employment either at the top or at the bottom of the socio-economic ladder.

Measuring social class by reference to income alone is fraught with difficulty, inaccuracy and misleading assumptions. A creative approach by Arbouch and Dadush (2019) uses car ownership in Morocco as an indicator of class through conspicuous consumption. The share of luxury cars registered in Morocco (predominantly Audi, BMW, Mercedes, Land Rover and Jeep) is just 6.9% of total registrations indicating that the number of Moroccans with incomes similar to affluent Europeans is small. In contrast, the middle class has three well-known preoccupations, access to good housing, education and healthcare. Many parents choose to send their children to costly private schools, many of which teach in French, a legacy of the Protectorate. Being able to pay for quality education and healthcare creates incentives for Moroccan women to become self-employed. In 2019, only 14% of 7 million Moroccan pupils were registered in private schools (Koundouno, 2019).

Two added layers of complexity in this social fabric are the hierarchy of respect attached to a family name in Morocco and the deep-seated loyalty to one's city or province of birth. Many family names are instantly recognisable such as those from Fes which convey a sense of upper-class standing or Berber names, which indicate region of origin. If individuals doing business together discover that their families originate from the same area, an immediate feeling of trust and solidarity develops even if their business takes place far from home. An inevitable result of these phenomena is the social networking and preference system known in French as *le tuyau* (pipeline) or *le piston* (piston) and elsewhere in the Arab world as *wasta* (clout or pull). WEs at all levels of Moroccan society must deal with this web of business influence and develop appropriate networking and negotiating skills.

In 2019, King Mohamed VI acknowledged the country's social disparities, recognised that past development plans have not reduced social and inter-regional disparities and called for private initiative and self-employment in rural tourism, commerce and local industry. The Programme for the Reduction of Territorial and Social Disparities is a seven-year programme (2017–2023) intended to benefit twelve million people by reducing disparities in access to public education, health, water and electricity (Ennaji, 2019). The Moroccan government aims to increase female employment to 30%, increase the number of women graduates from vocational education to 8% and promote a sustainable environment for the economic empowerment of women.

In 2021, Jamila El Moussali, Minister of Solidarity, Social Development and Equality confirmed that entrepreneurship is an essential tool to promote gender equality and women's empowerment. The Intelaka initiative of 2020 encourages entrepreneurship, particularly in the rural world. The 3-year $625 million Trust Fund was amplified with a $210 million contribution from the Hassan II Fund for Economic and Social Development to provide funding for young entrepreneurs to start their own businesses (*North Africa Post, 2020*).

Vignettes and the Gender-GEDI Framework (Aidis et al., 2013)

Real-life examples of WEs in Morocco demonstrate how external environmental factors and personal characteristics shape their lived experience. Factors include type of industry or commercial sector, scale and scope of operations, location, use of technology, operation as individuals or as members of collective organisations as well as personal demographics, values and objectives, types of skills and business readiness. Motivations to become self-employed vary from achieving financial independence to making lifestyle choices to contributing to civil society and sustainability.

Each vignette illustrates one of the 15 pillars in the Gender-GEDI framework in Exhibit 2.21. This approach necessarily simplifies each woman's experience of entrepreneurship because elements from several pillars are easily identifiable in each vignette. However, taken together, these examples paint a rich picture of women's entrepreneurship in Morocco. The objective of the Gender-GEDI study of women's entrepreneurship in seventeen countries was to identify the weakest 'pillar' in each country so that respective governments might concentrate attention on remedial action and innovation. The present analysis suggests that in the case of Morocco, increasing WEs' awareness of and access to financial assistance is the factor requiring most attention, followed by stronger community support and more effective preparation of all women for doing business.

Pillar 1: Opportunity Perception and Equal Legal Rights

In 2021, AFEM negotiated with the Moroccan Central Guarantee Fund to cover 80% of an investment loan for women's entrepreneurship projects (ID4D, 2016). Also, on International Women's Day in 2021, the Banque Centrale Populaire launched its new Gender Bond, a microfinance project

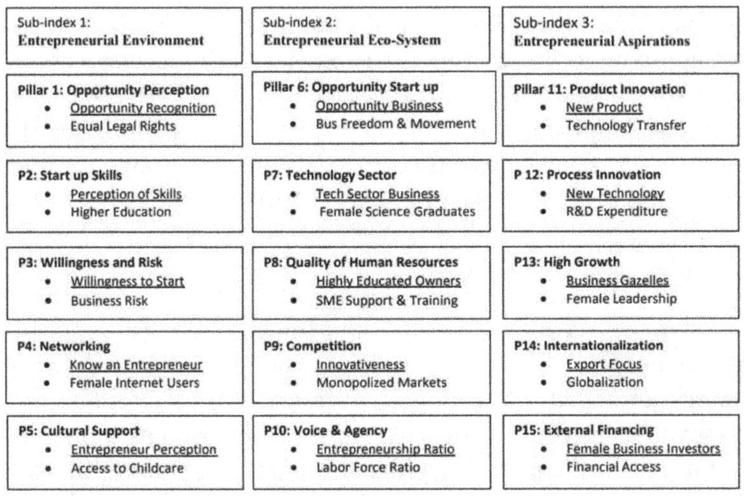

Exhibit 2.21 The Gender-GEDI framework (Aidis et al. 2013)

to improve women's financial independence and combat negative social pressures and lack of access to startup capital (Tyson, 2021). Gender-Responsive Budgeting (GRB) ensures that allocation of public resources promotes gender equality and women's empowerment while reducing poverty, exclusion and marginalisation.

GRB programmes developed by Morocco's Department of Literacy since 2009 report that 85% of the beneficiaries are women (Topping, 2015). For example, Fadma used public funds for literacy education: 'Before I was a housewife in charge of domestic work. One day I decided to change my life and I joined classes. For two years, I learned to read and write. I also learned Arabic, calligraphy and plastic arts. Today I create my own paintings and with the other women in my course, we decided to create a cooperative to better market our products' (UN Women, 2014).

Pillar 2: Start Up Skills

Camélia Drissi, an engineer in infrastructure projects, noticed that women were opening informal kitchen businesses, cooking, packing and selling home-cooked meals that may not conform to statutory hygiene standards. During a visit to the United States, Camélia learned about kitchen incubators like Union Kitchen in Washington DC and La Cocina in San Francisco and saw how this idea could work in Morocco. In 2016, Camélia created 'Spatula' offering women a shared-use kitchen space with affordable rent and flexible time schedules. Facilities include freezers, storage spaces, cooking equipment and a meeting room for training sessions. Women have access to a website with booking calendars and a link to crowdfunding. Technical support includes marketing, mentoring and networking. In 2016 Spatula was selected as a finalist in a Moroccan social entrepreneurship competition called Forsa-Challenge (Drissi, 2016).

Pillar 3: Willingness and Risk

Tourism is a key economic sector in Morocco, alongside agribusiness and manufacturing. The government's 'Vision 2020' aimed to position the country among the top 20 global destinations by doubling the size of the industry, creating infrastructure for 200,000 new beds, doubling foreign tourist numbers and tripling the number of domestic travellers. In 2019, tourist entries were almost 13 million including budget visitors (backpackers and adventure-seekers), cultural tourists, high-end hotel and resort guests and luxury desert campers. Tourists come from France,

Spain, Germany, the Netherlands, Italy and the UK, as well as Canada, the United States, Japan, China and Brazil (Roudies, 2010). Tourism offers women scope for self-employment through low cost of entry and use of home accommodations. WEs in Morocco host bed-and-breakfasts, rental holiday homes ('gîtes') and luxury 'riads' typical of the renovated historic homes in Marrakesh and Tangiers.

When Zina Bencheikh became general manager at adventure travel company PEAK DMC's Marrakesh office in 2017, the company had fifty tour leaders and not one was female. Tour leading was not considered suitable employment for women due to negative perceptions of sexual harassment and perceived physical dangers. According to Zina, 'The nature of the job means you are travelling away from home and in the company of foreign tourists… [At that time] only four percent of tour leaders in Morocco were female and of these, very few spoke English, a primary requirement in tourism in Morocco…The industry in Morocco is well regulated with the number of guides limited by the number of licences issued by the government. This means demand often exceeds supply therefore guides are well paid, compared to many other jobs'. In 2018, Zina lobbied the Moroccan Ministry of Tourism and succeeded in having tour guide licences issued to women. 'We wanted to get as many women to apply as we could, so I encouraged all the women in the office and from my network to apply and even helped them with their paperwork. We had five women pass the test'. There are now 13 female tour leaders in the company, opening possibilities for offering women-only tours (Christine, 2019).

Unfortunately, tourism and transportation intersect in Morocco with the problem of sexual harassment. In 2017, Naima, a former self-employed taxi driver commented: 'When I worked as a taxi driver, I often heard criticisms and insults from my male colleagues; one of them told me to go knead bread and prepare lunch. This work is not for women, go home'. As one of only a few women taxi drivers in Marrakesh, Naima had many female clients who preferred to ride with her as a woman. However, she eventually quit her job due to harassment and social pressure (UN Women, 2017).

Pillar 4: Networking and Female Internet Users

Women artisans in isolated rural areas in the Atlas Mountains find solidarity and assistance through cooperative ventures while women doing business in cities co-create and co-manage websites together. They use e-commerce to promote their own merchandise and services or as a marketplace for products sourced nationally across Morocco. DHL, FedEx and UPS operate in urban areas alongside the national express postal service, Chronoposte, but control over timing of 'last-mile delivery' depends on the local shipper and delays are common. The unique selling proposition of these cyber-stores is not speed of service but range, quality and authenticity of merchandise labelled 'Made in Morocco'. The social mission of serving and promoting WEs in Morocco is a common motivation for this type of women-owned cyber-store.

Magali, Selma and Inès operate Chic-Intemporel, an online store offering a wide range of organic personal care products, jewellery and home décor such as candles and rugs produced by Moroccan artisans. Combining business and social entrepreneurship, their mission is three-fold: to support local craftspeople and cooperatives; promote high-quality traditional items; and operate in a socially responsible, ethical and sustainable manner. Goals are to improve working conditions and promote women's empowerment while respecting the ecosystem and biodiversity. In 2021, Chic-Intemporel partnered with an international hotel in Casablanca to host a fair exhibiting a range of nationally sourced products that were also advertised on Facebook (chic-intemporel.com/fr/team, 2021).

Pillar 5: Cultural Support and Childcare

Forbes magazine's 2021 list of the Middle East's Power Businesswomen featured four Moroccan women: Nezha Hayat (8th), Salwa Idrissi Akhannouch (19th) (see Pillar 13 in the following), Rita Maria Zniber (33rd) and Miriem Bensalah Chaqroun (36th) (Hatim, 2021b).

Rita Zniber is Chairman and CEO of Diana Holdings, Africa's largest wines and spirits company and Morocco's top wine producer. This family company has been operating for four decades in olive growing, poultry farming, trade and distribution. Rita is founder of the Rita Zniber Foundation, a non-profit organisation that cares for abandoned children in the context of the Rights of the Child. Two facilities, 'Le Nid' (the nest) and the 'Annexe du Nid' adjacent to a hospital in Meknes host 300 orphaned newborn babies. The Foundation manages adoptions and fostering, provides vaccinations and help with schoolwork, runs holiday camps for children of ages 8–15 and hosts group outings and birthday parties for adolescents (fondationritazniber.org/fr/historique).

Pillar 6: Opportunity Startup

Argan nuts grow on trees in forests around Essaouira and Agadir and the oil, 'liquid gold', was traditionally used for dipping bread. Adding to the product's long time success, foreign tourists have been buying directly from local producers and this created global marketing opportunities across numerous product categories such as lotions, lip-glosses, shampoos, soaps, medical applications, aromatherapy, food and home cleaning products. Production increased exponentially, positioning Morocco as the world's leading exporter. Argan oil has been endorsed by celebrities such as Kim Kardashian and Catherine Zeta-Jones (Mebtoul, 2020a).

Income from argan oil production supports over 2 million people in the region called the Arganeraie, a UNESCO Biosphere Reserve and a Globally Important Agricultural Heritage System. The oil is painstakingly produced by hand by Berber women to preserve quality (Degen, 2022; Chapter 1, this volume). The women work in 50 unionised cooperatives which receive support from the Mohamed VI Foundation for Research and Protection of the Argan Tree and international organisations such as Canada's International Development Research Centre and the European Commission. Training is also funded by grants from the Canadian, Japanese and United Kingdom embassies and the diplomatic corps accredited to Morocco; Oxfam-Québec; the Comité d'Entraide Internationale; and private Moroccan citizens (IDRC, 2010).

Assistance involves shop set up, equipment purchase, bottle purchasing, design and production of labels. Training includes production methods, management, accounting and literacy. Social outcomes include increasing women's awareness of their rights, reforestation of argan forests and promotion of tourism. Marketing cooperation with hotels and tour operators is expected to increase sales by 50% and photographs of goats climbing argan trees are well-known images used to promote tourism in Morocco.

Many women in the Arganeraie have become family breadwinners, able to fund education for themselves and their children. Amina Bouna, manager at the Marjana Coopérative described the empowerment achieved by the women: 'We have all types of women here — young, old, married and divorced… Before, they made the oil at home. Their husbands sold it on the market and kept the money. Now they don't need their husbands' money because they make their own. It's a win-win situation' (Rosengren,

2020). However, wages remain below the national minimum and mechanical extraction is now halving costs of hand-made oil by sacrificing quality for price. Recognising the negative economic impact on workers, global cosmetics company L'Oréal has pledged to source all its argan oil from cooperatives that sign up to the principles of Fair Trade (see cooperativet oudarte.com).

Pillar 7: Technology Sector and Female Science Graduates

Nazik El Yaalaoui has an MSc in engineering, an MBA and eighteen years of professional experience. She speaks four languages and is Country Director in Morocco for the International Youth Foundation. 'In Morocco, the gender who goes beyond high school? It's women. All the engineering schools have more than 80% young women. They might wear scarves, or they might not, but they are women. In med school, the majority are women' (McCormick, 2016).

In 2018 UNESCO reported that 42.2% of Moroccan graduates from engineering faculties were women. 44.2% were in agriculture, 72.3% in health and social sciences, 48.7% in natural sciences and 41.3% in technology and communication sciences. However, career path development for women scientists and engineers remains problematic. Even if they find positions in appropriate industries, many women discover that promotion is blocked by prejudice or discrimination, leading them to move into other fields or become entrepreneurs (Zahir, 2021). A notable path to financial independence for women health science graduates is ownership or management of a private pharmacy.

Souhad Azennoud is a founding member of the women's Ariaf Coopérative in Ghafsai in the Rif Mountains. She is a pioneer of agro-ecology and received first prize at the Terre de Femmes Maroc ceremony in 2016. Her work is linked to UN SDG 13 (climate change) and SDG 15 (preservation of mountain ecosystems and biodiversity for sustainable development). According to Souhad, 'If women earn a good living, they will stay in the countryside. Otherwise, they will urge their family to leave. We cannot act alone; we need to come together! I belong to one agricultural cooperative and I have founded others: I encourage people and women to work together…But climate change is a global phenomenon: the whole world needs to work together!' (Azennoud, 2016).

Facing threats to their olive harvests from climate change, the Ariaf Coopérative diversified into animal husbandry, trade, crafts and tourism. When weekly regional markets closed during the COVID-19 pandemic, members turned to e-commerce using the ADS Coopsclub platform to negotiate product delivery fees with service providers (see coopsclub. com). This platform was developed in 2020 by the Ministry of Solidarity, Social Development, Equality and Family as a marketplace for women's cooperatives (UN Women, 2020). Under the English language banner 'The Power of Social Marketing', the bilingual (French/Arabic) website delivers products nationwide, guarantees returns, provides 24/7 service support and offers members rewards.

Fadwa Moussaif and Amal Kenzari, co-founders of IDYR Design, met at university where Fadwa specialised in design and marketing and Amal studied industry and environment. They created a social enterprise to promote three goals: ethics in business by employing women artisans, environmental protection through recycling of materials and preservation of traditional skills of weaving and leatherwork (idyrdesign.com/en). It was Fadwa's university project that grew into the concept for IDYR Design producing handmade Boucherouite rugs. These are woven into modern designs using old clothes (fabric, wool or leather) and recycled thread discarded by factories. Valued for its weight and protection against the cold, the Boucherouite rug also serves as a blanket or simple decoration and is used by bus and taxi drivers as seat coverings. The name IDYR is Berber Tamazight meaning 'the living' and the logo is a motif used by women of the Atlas Mountains for tattoos symbolising strength and independence.

At university Fadwa learned that Moroccan women artisans sell their products at very low prices to dealers who profit by selling directly to tourists. She also discovered that Morocco's textile industry throws away 205,000 tonnes of fabric every year and only 8% of unwanted materials is recycled. 'These women only needed an opportunity to show their skills and to express themselves. They did not know how to promote their talents and generate income…. I am realizing my childhood dream of supporting social and environmental causes. I always wanted to do something to sustainably help people in precarious situations but I never knew how until I reached university… My parents, my sister and my brother were my first investors, incubators, clients, counsellors and supporters when I decided to venture into entrepreneurship' (Hatim, 2020).

Pillar 8: Quality of Human Resources and Highly Educated Owners

The Moroccan caftan is a traditional long dress that is beautifully embroidered and matched with a stiff wide belt that is heavily ornamented and may be made of carved gold. The caftan has great symbolic value conveying personal elegance, social standing and glamour. Four styles are named after the places of origin: Rabat, Meknes, Fes and the Tangiers/Tetouan region.

Salima El Boussouni grew up in a family-owned sewing school in Casablanca. After graduating from HEC Montreal, the Montreal Academy of Arts and Design and the leading Moroccan business school ISCAE, Salima became a stylist, combining traditional forms of the caftan with contemporary cuts, colours, fabrics and decoration. In 2015 she was a finalist in CAFTAN, the annual fashion event organised by the Moroccan women's magazine *Femmes du Maroc*. Under the brand-name 'Caftan Skalli', Salima's collections have been presented in Paris, New York, Dubai, Lisbon, Milan, Beirut, Geneva and Kuwait City. Salima markets her creations internationally through her website (caftan-skalli.com) and social media and has a retail operation in Morocco Mall in Casablanca (Toum-Benchekroun, 2021).

Pillar 9: Competition and Innovativeness

Visual artist Asmaa Benachir founded her social enterprise 'Au Grain de Sésame' in 2007 to combine art with sustainable development of art and crafts (augraindesesame.org). Her business combines a literary café, gallery and training centre where women learn how to produce and sell their own recycled and upcycled paper art, thereby achieving financial independence. 'I'm an artist, so things are different. Art is open for women here in Morocco… I think it's more difficult for women to be in a position of decision, like a man. I think it's not impossible because we have women as directors of very big national companies but there are few'. In 2013 Asmaa won a SEED Award for Entrepreneurship in Sustainable Development under the UNDP Initiative for the Environment and was a semi-finalist in 2015 for the African Award for Entrepreneurship (Sang, 2018).

Pillar 10: Voice and Agency

In 2011 Fatima Ouakhoum organised the Women's Cooperative of Imghlaus in the southern Atlas Mountains. Based on the principle of communal action, revenues are shared amongst members. In future the Cooperative hopes to build a new centre and move out of their one room workshop without electricity. The Cooperative's products include traditional deep-pile Beni Ourain Berber rugs (made from natural wool and dyes), flatweave kilim rugs and blankets. Recognisable by its beige background and black or brown symmetrical line designs, the Beni Ourain style of rug is usually associated with the northeastern Atlas region. However, many of the southern Imelghaus women trace their Berber heritage through marriage, motivating the Cooperative to include this style in its product range. The Cooperative hosts a website featuring photos of each woman involved in production of an item. Prices range from a few hundred US dollars to thousands and each item is identified by its designer's name and the number of women working on it (theanou.com/store/19-imelghas-womens-cooperative-imelghas-morocco).

Pillar 11: Product Innovation and Technology Transfer

Women make up almost half of the rural labour force, usually in low paid, informal employment, often as seasonal labourers picking, packing and processing fruit, vegetables, nuts and olives. Although Morocco's national labour law regulates the agricultural sector and sets minimum wage and maximum hours of work, many rural workers do not benefit from these protections due to a lack of enforcement.

The UN Entity for Gender Equality and the Empowerment of Women supports cooperatives of women seed growers in Morocco through joint action with the local NGO Terre et Humanisme. Training is provided in managing seed quality, improving production through agro-ecology and business commercialisation skills. By 2016, 203 trained women seed growers were managing three seed banks. Sustainable farming tailored to local conditions allows these WEs to mitigate the effects of global climate change on their crops (UN Women, 2021).

Pillar 12: Process Innovation

One hundred women living in eight desert oases in Errachidia on the eastern side of the Middle Atlas cultivate medicinal and aromatic plants (MAPs) using renewable energy and conservation methods based on traditional knowledge. The Annama Association for the Development of Rural Women unites 12 cooperatives and 15 NGOs in the fight against poverty through sustainable development. Initially the group planted seeds on a hectare of land using drip irrigation and a solar pump. After only two years, incomes started to rise. The Association bought a second hectare of land and plans to share the group's experience with neighbouring communities. According to the Association's President, 'The women work hard and are struggling for a more dignified life' (UN Women, 2015).

The women's Coopérative Tudert in Essaoiura province on the coast also harvests MAPs, selling to health food, groceries, cosmetic stores, herbalists, delicatessen and mass merchandisers. During the COVID-19 lockdowns, like other cooperatives, Tudert turned to online marketing through the *ADS Coopsclub. Financial support from UN Women is part of an economic empowerment project funded by the Coca-Cola Foundation to strengthen rural women's leadership as change agents while preserving biodiversity* (UN Women, 2020).

Pillar 13: High Growth — Business Gazelles and Female Leadership

Born in Casablanca, Salwa Idrissi Akhannouch is from a Berber family in the mountains southeast of Agadir. Salwa is wife of Aziz Akhannouch, a billionaire businessman and politician who has served as Minister of Agriculture since 2007. Her business ventures typify 'gazelles', young fast-growing companies which maintain rapid expansion of employment and sales for at least four years. Salwa inherited a fortune from her grandfather who held a monopoly in the tea business in Morocco in the 1960s. She became an entrepreneur in 1993 starting a company to distribute flooring materials, followed by franchising the Zara brand in 2004 and the Massimo Dutti brand in 2006 (Anastasia, 2020).

Salwa is founder and CEO of the Aksal-Morocco Mall Group which specialises in luxury goods, department stores and shopping malls. The Aksal Group owns 50% of the Morocco Mall in Casablanca built in 2007 at a cost of $240 million. It is one of the largest retail centres in Africa, has 15 million annual visitors and generates revenues of $514 million. Aksal owns sole franchise rights to brands sold in the Mall and across Morocco including Zara, Banana Republic, Fendi, Gucci, Ralph Lauren, Massimo Dutti, Pull & Bear, Gap and Galéries Lafayette. Salwa is also founder of the cosmetics brand Yan & One and head of her husband's Akwa Group, a major distributor of petroleum products under the brand name Afriquia. In 2015 Salwa ranked eighth on *Arabian Business*'s list of the 100 Most Influential Arab Women, in 2018 she ranked second among the 50 Most

Influential Businesswomen in Africa and was included on *Forbes Middle East* magazine's 2020 list of 'Women Behind Middle Eastern Brands'.

Pillar 14: Internationalisation

Rahma Al Mouden tells a 'rags to riches' story, becoming a successful entrepreneur in the Netherlands and being named 'Dutch Businesswoman of the Year' in 1999 by the European Federation of Black Women Business Owners. Born in Tangiers, Rahma started work in 1977 as a cleaner at the Municipal Energy Company in Amsterdam. She founded the Multicultural Amsterdam Cleaning Company which serves the cleaning, hotel, catering, security and maintenance sectors as well as construction property management. It has 500 employees and offices in The Hague, Rotterdam and Amsterdam. Since 2016 Rahma has been guiding children with learning difficulties at Orion College in Amsterdam, providing business training, role models and work visits (Wikipedia, 2021b).

Pillar 15: Financial Access

Sana Afouaiz founded the Womenpreneur Initiative, an NGO based in Belgium that helps women in North Africa start and grow their own businesses (womenpreneur-initiative.com). Since 2016 her organisation has supported 10,000 women through mentoring, networking, leadership and technology programmes. 'When it comes to Morocco, a country where I grew up myself, the challenges are different. You have the economic difficulties — less economic investors who take you seriously. There are cultural issues — as a female entrepreneur you have certain limits. For example, being a female entrepreneur means working late, travelling around and so on. However, programmes like the Gender Bond can make all the difference by putting capital directly into the hands of female entrepreneurs'.

An Integrating Opinion

These vignettes illustrate the diversity of Moroccan WEs' motivations, skills, resources, sectors of operation, type of organisation and levels of success. All vary as a function of location, access to funding, attitudes toward women in the business environment and prevailing market conditions. This commentary by Safaa Nhairy (edited for space) lays the groundwork for the following SWOT analysis (Nhairy, 2017).

'Here are the lessons I wish someone would have shared with me when I first launched my business in Morocco. I organised short meetings, dispatched tasks and explained to each person what was expected of them. Then I would come back to find that nothing had been done according to plan, even with qualified people who had graduated from well-known schools. I learned I had to keep following up over and over again.

Suppliers can be your worst enemies. You need to constantly make sure that work is in progress and there are no unforeseen problems with the order. If you don't, they will assume the project is not that important and will turn their attention to handling projects from people who ARE putting the pressure on… In Morocco 'I'll get back to you in a bit' could mean days or weeks or months. It depends on who said it and how they were feeling. No matter what the business is, regardless of the individual's position or title, deadlines are left up in the air.

While quite proficient at using apps such as WhatsApp, IMO and Messenger, Moroccan professionals can sometimes be very annoying—such as when you give someone a call, leave a message and they never get back to you or when you send them an email and they don't acknowledge receiving it. I have learned that if you call twice and you still don't get a response, chances are that the person you're calling is avoiding you.

It is not part of Moroccan culture to thank, congratulate or provide feedback. In some cases, a client decides to work with another company without explaining the decision. Without feedback, I could never know whether the problem was due to my fees, my service, the quality of the work or an incident with one of my employees. In Morocco, giving negative feedback is viewed as taking a risk. One never knows what might happen in the future or when your paths might cross again. Positive feedback could be used against you if the project ultimately fails.

Job applicants show up late for interview without any apology or excuse. Meetings are cancelled 30 minutes before time or the person simply isn't there. Phone calls take place routinely during meetings. Usually, people don't have a clear objective or outcome in mind and meetings may last hours, due to lack of agenda, bad time management and careless transcription of minutes. Being properly prepared allows you to lead the discussion.

In Morocco everything is 'urgent', most likely due to a lack of organisation, anticipation, planning or prioritisation. Moroccan culture is more about hours spent on the job than about productivity or results achieved and meetings scheduled late in the day are intended as evidence of working hard. Whether it involves administration, personnel, suppliers or clients, there is always a reason why it's not ready yet.

In business meetings, actual business is only discussed about 20% of the time. The other 80% is dedicated to finding commonalities, people we know, places we have been to, etc. In other words, you must find like-minded people if you want to grow your business. Recommendations and referrals are the only way by which you can progress. Who you know and how you could be useful in the eyes of your interlocutor are key. '*Bak saahbi*' ('Your Dad is my friend') means that only personal connections and friendships, recommendations and favours work for everything from small projects to large tenders. Connections are what Moroccans swear by. Networking events are not used to meet future colleagues, business partners or investors. Only trusted people, such as friends and family members, provide recommendations. Gifts and presents are part of daily business life in Morocco but people do not talk about it openly. Buyers for many companies are primarily interested in what is in it for them before they examine how it can benefit their company'. The next section presents a SWOT analysis.

Toward the Future

Strengths of WEs in Morocco

Women of all demographics and regions of Morocco are motivated to become entrepreneurs to escape poverty and dependency on male relatives; to build a career based on personal skills, higher education or artistic creativity; to serve a social purpose relating to quality-of-life such as climate change and sustainability; or simply to help others. Creativity and ability among Moroccan women cover the spectrum including traditional arts and crafts, fashion and design, agribusiness, science, e-commerce, organisational skill, financial management and languages. WEs understand the value of brand-name marketing reflecting their regional or tribal identity or ethical positioning and recognise the power of the country-of-origin label 'Made in Morocco'.

A substantial cohort of women actively lobbies to bring about legislative changes to promote gender equality in business and entrepreneurship. Other women provide mentoring, networking and business training to WEs, sharing their experience as executives in Moroccan companies, government and civil society organisations. Women members of government and NGOs are creating and supporting targeted programmes in start-up financing, business methods and marketing. Finally, inter-generational family members and domestic employees provide childcare for WEs.

Weaknesses of WEs in Morocco

WEs recognise their deficits in business knowledge, skills, contacts and lack of ability to 'work the system'. Inadequate public education leaves women poorly prepared to act as businesswomen and even women graduates are often unaware of support systems offered by the government, NGOs or business institutions. This is due to poor marketing and ineffective implementation of such programmes.

Lack of production facilities outside the home, lack of land or supplies, lack of office space or access to the internet are all aggravated by WEs' persistent problem of lack of knowledge about or access to funding. Women have ideas and ambitions but infrastructure in the entrepreneurial ecosystem is not yet articulated in a way that effectively helps those it is designed to serve.

Other challenges arise from Moroccan culture itself. As a collectivist culture, it is important to 'know and be known' to function effectively in business. Networking and cooperation among women are valuable support mechanisms but WEs must build and use contacts with men in their business sector. Endemic corruption, unfair practises, bribery, harassment and lack of transparency make business difficult for everyone in Morocco but have much more severe impact on women, especially those trying to do business as individual entrepreneurs.

WEs who build their business on ethical values must work with business customs shaped by French and Arab culture. Problems include time management, reliability, efficiency, accountability and honesty in business. Childcare is a constraint on WEs who are primarily responsible for children's welfare within the family. The lack of public or commercial childcare and the high cost of this service are continuing problems and WEs must find their own solutions.

WEs face the challenge of the 'unknown unknown', not knowing that they do not know about support services and funding opportunities available to them. The government has recognised the value of entrepreneurship and new legislation, financing and support programmes are being launched. However, these are often inadequately promoted or implemented and outcomes are not measured. Lack of coordination, integration and effective reach is endemic in emerging economies where public administration is inadequate to 'make things happen' or 'happen properly'. In the meantime, professional associations, NGOs and women's lobbying groups carry the burden of outreach to WEs especially through word-of-mouth and social media.

Opportunities for WEs in Morocco

In 2020, the European Investment Bank and Morocco's Al Amana Microfinance signed a loan agreement of €3 million to support development of 11,560 micro-enterprises with a target of 45% women beneficiaries (Kasraoui, 2020). The Imtiaz, Moussadana and Istitmar programmes managed by the National Agency for the Promotion of Small and Medium Enterprises also provide investment subsidies to entrepreneurs. However, Erghai (2014) commented that 'The Imtiaz programme for high-potential companies has helped 170 companies for some $68 million, but eligibility criteria are too strict…. The last five years have proved that development of an ecosystem for tech companies also requires the development of a community, through interaction and events'.

Two online platforms, Wuluj and Cotizi, offer start-ups a solution to the persistent problem of funding through crowdfunding. Weetracker Research presents 'a comprehensive map of all the key players involved in shaping the Moroccan start up ecosystem' including incubators, accelerators, government-led initiatives, ecosystem builders, start-up communities, media, angel and venture funds (Team Weetracker, 2018). These include INJAZ Al Maghreb, ENACTUS, Start Up Your Life, StartUp Maroc, MCISE (Moroccan Centre for Innovation and Social Entrepreneurship), Phosboucraa Foundation (the corporate social responsibility service of OCP, Morocco's largest producer of phosphates), The British Council, the World Bank, the US Embassy in Morocco, foreign governments and civil society organisations such as the International Youth Foundation's YouthActionNet global network.

While Weetracker's list is impressive in its coverage, it would be difficult for WEs with little business knowledge to know which programme is appropriate to their needs, or how to approach one of these organisations, or even that the Weetracker list exists. A hard-hitting evaluation of efforts to help entrepreneurs in Morocco by (Erghai, 2014) concluded: 'Young entrepreneurs need mentorship and follow-up more than funds. The digital economy start-ups need incubators, technological hubs and accelerators to become a vector of social and economic improvement. As for the entrepreneurs, they should know by now that they cannot depend on public funds and the support of the government, as money will always arrive later than planned'.

Threats Affecting WEs in Morocco

During the COVID-19 pandemic, MCISE used a hybrid formula (online and face-to-face) to ensure continuity of its educational, training and mentoring programmes. In 2020 MCISE launched a fundraising campaign on Wuluj, #s'entraider_pour_aider ('help each other to help'), targeting entrepreneurs impacted by the national lockdown (Mebtoul, 2020b).

WEs in Morocco face competition on each element of the marketing mix. Aggressive low-price competition from Chinese retailers selling products 'Made in China' threatens WEs operating in the big cities. Mechanised production of argan oil threatens the labour-intensive business model of women's cooperatives in the Arganeraie by producing more volume at lower cost. Synthetic carpets and rugs sold in modern malls compete on quality and price with the hand-made artisanal work of Berber women in isolated mountain cooperatives. Efficient e-commerce platforms promote, sell and deliver hand-made crafts worldwide, competing with local craftswomen who rely on sales to tourists visiting their remote places of production. Strongly promoted online brand-name products benefit from a more sophisticated image and higher prices than equivalent items sold simply under the name of a tribe or a region. E-commerce requires linguistic and technical proficiency to host a multi-lingual platform, quote prices in several currencies and ensure safe online payments. Finally, fulfilment of delivery of orders is hampered in Morocco by an underdeveloped express package delivery industry.

The future for WEs in Morocco looks promising, despite significant challenges. As an emerging economy, the country is building strength in research and design, investing in manufacturing and exporting, modernising the entrepreneurial ecosystem, updating the legal and financial infrastructure, expanding tourism, promoting sustainability and attracting FDI across a range of industries. Morocco's country image is positive and the nation is building presence on the global stage. Yet despite all these country advantages, the personal strengths of WEs are under stress as they try to take advantage of market opportunities. A persistent informational and organisational gap remains in Morocco between providers of services, resources and funding and their targeted WEs. In 2018 WEs numbered less than 10,000, representing only 10% of total enterprises (Asli and Habiba Bensassi, 2018).

Exhibit 2.22 Entrepreneurs of the future; photograph © Léo-Paul Dana

A comprehensive and sustained national marketing campaign by leading government agencies is urgently needed to inform WEs of available resources, facilitate uptake and build community. Also, the overarching problem of inefficient cultural business practices in Morocco undermines each woman's best efforts, especially the persistent climate of corruption, personal preference, lack of transparency and gender discrimination. Social marketing campaigns are needed to educate the nation about best practices. In the future, improved articulation of the business ecosystem will trigger major economic opportunities for Morocco as a nation and will benefit the country's youth (Exhibit 2.22) and its many WEs immeasurably.

References

Aidis, R., J. Weeks, L. Szerb, Z. J. Acs, and A. Lloyd (2013, April), *The 2013 Gender Global Entrepreneurship and Development index (GEDI): Executive Report (April)*, Washington, DC: Produced by the Global Entrepreneurship and Development Institute. DOI: 10.13140/RG. 2.1.3619.9766

Akl, Z. (2020, June 28), "The Berbers of Morocco: A Culture Under Challenge," https://news.cgtn.com/news/2020-06-28/The-Berbers-of-Morocco-A-culture-under-challenge-RGONdj9cas/index.html

Amine, L. S., and K. Staub (2008), Women Entrepreneurs in Sub-Saharan Africa: An Institutional Theory Analysis from a Social Marketing Point of View. *Entrepreneurship & Regional Development: An International Journal* 21 (2), pp. 183–211. https://www.tandfonline.com/doi/abs/10.1080/08985620802182144

Anastasia, N. C. (2020, October 19), "Salwa Idrissi Akhannouch Biography," https://urbanwomanmag.com/salwa-idrissi-akhannouch-biography/

Arab News (2020, December 13), "Moroccan Schools to Teach Jewish History and Culture," https://www.reuters.com/article/us-israel-usa-morocco-idUSKBN28L2HG

Arbouch, M., and U. Dadush (2019), *Measuring the Middle Class in the World and in Morocco.* Rabat, Morocco: Policy Centre for the New South. https://www.policycenter.ma/sites/default/files/PP%20-%2019-09%20%28%20Uri%20Dadush%29_0.pdf

Ardant, P. (1974, March 15), "Vingt ans de coopération culturelle et technique avec le Maroc: Echec ou réussite?" https://aan.mmsh.univ-aix.fr/Pdf/AAN-1974-13_21.pdf

Asli, A., and N. Habiba Bensassi (2018), "Female Entrepreneurship in Morocco, Obstacles and Ways to Overcome Them," Paper Presented to the Governance Research and Development Centre, April 13–14, Dubrovnik, Croatia. https://www.econstor.eu/bitstream/10419/180004/1/ofel-2018-p390-401.pdf

Azennoud, S. (2016, June 2), "From Where I Stand: Souhad Azennoud," https://www.unwomen.org/en/news/stories/2016/6/from-where-i-stand-souhad-azennoud

Barger, B. (2019, February 24), "Princess Lalla Salma of Morocco–The first Moroccan Consort to be Publicly Acknowledged," https://www.historyofroyalwomen.com/morocco/who-is-lalla-salma-moroccos-missing-princess/

Bennis, S. (2012, April 2), "Morocco and Spain: History of a Contentious Relationship," https://www.moroccoworldnews.com/2012/04/33540/morocco-and-spain-history-of-a-contentious-relationship/

Bouzekraoui, H., and D. Ferhane (2017), "An Exploratory Study of Women's Entrepreneurship in Morocco," *Journal of Entrepreneurship: Research & Practice* 2017, 869458. https://ibimapublishing.com/articles/JERP/2017/869458/869458.pdf

Brush, C., I. E. Allen, A. de Bruin, and F. Welter (2010), "Gender Embeddedness of Women Entrepreneurs: An Empirical Test of the 5 'M' Framework. (Summary) Exhibit 1," https://www.researchgate.net/publication/235966679_GENDER_EMBEDDEDNESS_OF_WOMEN_ENTREPRENEURS_AN_EMPIRICAL_TEST_OF_THE_5_M_FRAMEWORK_SUMMARY/figures

Cateora, P., J. Graham, M. Gilly, and B. Money (2020), *International Marketing*, 18th ed., New York, NY: McGraw-Hill Higher Education.

Christine, T. (2019, November 27), "The Woman Who Challenged Morocco's Tourism Industry for Women's Rights — And Won," https://www.forbes.com/sites/theresachristine/2019/11/27/the-woman-who-challenged-moroccos-tourism-industry-for-womens-rights-and-won/?sh=60acecfe594c

Chtatou, M. (2019, September 5), "Expulsion of Sephardic Jews from Spain in 1492 and their Relocation and Success in Morocco—Analysis," https://www.eurasiareview.com/05092019-expulsion-of-sephardic-jews-from-spain-in-1492-and-their-relocation-and-success-in-morocco-analysis/

CIA World Factbook (2021), "Morocco: People and Society," https://www.cia.gov/the-world-factbook/countries/morocco/#people-and-society

CMES (Centre for Middle Eastern Studies) (2021), "The Culture and Arts of Morocco and the Berbers," https://cmes.arizona.edu/sites/cmes.arizona.edu/files/The%20Culture%20and%20Arts%20of%20Morocco%20and%20the%20Berbers.pdf

Dana, L.-P. (2006), "Business Values among the Imazighen," *EuroMed Journal of Business* 1(2), pp. 82–91. http://dx.doi.org/10.1108/14502190610750180

Dana, L.-P., and T. E. Dana (2008), "Ethnicity and Entrepreneurship in Morocco: A Photo-Ethnographic Study," *International Journal of Business and Globalisation* 2(3), pp. 209–226. https://www.inderscienceonline.com/doi/abs/10.1504/IJBG.2008.017677

Degen, A. A. (2022), "Indigenous Women in North Africa: Amazigh Women and Argan Oil," in L.-P. Dana, D. M. Nziku, R. Palalic, and V. Ramadani, eds., *Women's Entrepreneurship in North Africa: Historical Framework, Ecosystem, and Future Perspectives for the Region*, Singapore: World Scientific Publishing.

Drissi, C. (2016, February 22), "Spatula Supporting Women Kitchen Entrepreneurs in Morocco," https://thesolutionsjournal.com/2016/02/22/spatula-supporting-women-kitchen-entrepreneurs-in-morocco/

Dumpis, T. (2021a, January 29), "ONDH: 28.5% of Young People are not in Education, Employment, Training," https://www.moroccoworld news.com/2021/01/333680/ondh-28-5-of-young-people-are-not-in-education-employment-training/

Dumpis, T. (2021b, February 2), "Foreign Ministers of Morocco, Israel Talk Bilateral Cooperation," https://www.moroccoworldnews.com/2021/02/333942/foreign-ministers-of-morocco-israel-talk-bilateral-cooperation/

Dumpis, T. (2021c, March 10), "Moroccan-American Developing a Universal COVID-19 Vaccine," https://www.moroccoworldnews.com/2021/03/337010/moroccan-american-developing-a-universal-covid-19-vaccine/

Eljechtimi, A., and A. Rabinovitch (2020, December 11), "As Israel and Moroccan Jews Celebrate New Ties, Others are Critical," https://www.reuters.com/article/us-israel-usa-morocco-idUSKBN28L2HG

Ennaji, K. (2019, August 20), "King Mohammed VI Addresses Social Disparities in King and People's Revolution Speech," https://www.moroccoworldnews.com/2019/08/280752/king-mohammed-vi-social-disparities-king-people-revolution-speech/

Ennaji, M. (2021, January 9), "The US-Morocco-Israel Agreement and the Triumph of Pragmatism," https://www.moroccoworldnews.com/2021/01/331436/the-us-morocco-israel-agreement-and-the-triumph-of-pragmatism/

Erghai, M. (2014, December 29), "What Have Eight of Morocco's Support Organisations for Tech Entrepreneurship Achieved?" https://www.wamda.com/2014/12/tech-entrepreneurship-support-organisations-results

Euromed Rights (2012, October 10), "The Moroccan Family Code (Moudawana)," https://euromedrights.org/publication/the-moroccan-family-code-moudawana/

Ford Foundation (2019, February), "The Benefits of Collective Bargaining for Women: A Case Study of Morocco," https://www.fordfoundation.org/media/4551/the-benefits-of-collective-bargaining-for-women-a-case-study-of-morocco219.pdf

Fresh Fruit Portal (2021, March 3), "'Brexit Buster' Direct Shipping Route Announced Between UK and Morocco," https://www.freshfruitportal.com/news/2021/03/03/brexit-buster-direct-route-announced-between-uk-and-morocco/

Haaretz (2020, December 11), "U.S. Considering $3 billion in Morocco Investments after Israel Deal, Report Says," https://www.haaretz.com/middle-east-news/u-s-considering-3-billion-in-morocco-investments-after-israel-deal-report-says-1.9365988

Hallward, M., and C. Stewart (2018), "Challenges and Opportunities Facing Successful Women in Morocco," *Journal of North African Studies,* 23 (5), pp. 871–895. https://doi.org/10.1080/13629387.2017.1422980

Hammond, J. (2017, March 1), "Morocco is Actively Courting More Chinese Investment and Closer Ties," https://thediplomat.com/2017/03/morocco-chinas-gateway-to-africa/

Hatim, Y. (2020, July 30), "IDYR: The Art of Moroccan Boucherouite Meets Eco-Consciousness," https://www.moroccoworldnews.com/2020/07/313144/idyr-the-art-of-moroccan-boucherouite-meets-eco-consciousness/

Hatim, Y. (2021a, January 18), "Samir Bennis: Morocco Needs to End Language Barriers to Attract Investments," https://www.moroccoworldnews.com/2021/01/332304/samir-bennis-morocco-needs-to-end-language-barriers-to-attract-investments/

Hatim, Y. (2021b, February 9), "Four Moroccans Among 'Most Powerful Businesswomen' in Middle East,'" https://www.moroccoworldnews.com/2021/02/334439/4-moroccans-among-most-powerful-business women-in-middle-east/?fbclid=IwAR38x2rNM8RHLddCbmvRkhlIc ixKID7RCsyDAnV4ivfyYKrp_nGeB_BrCNk

Hatim, Y. (2021c, February 18), "Tiznit-Dakhla Highway in Southern Morocco Risks Running Behind Schedule," https://www.moroccoworldnews.com/2021/02/335327/tiznit-dakhla-highway-in-southern-morocco-risks-running-behind-schedule/

Hofstede-Insights (2021), "Morocco," https://www.hofstede-insights.com/country/morocco/

ID4D (Identification for Development: The World Bank) (2016, December 20). "More and More Women Entrepreneurs in Morocco," https://ideas4development.org/en/start-ups-women-morocco/

IDRC (International Development Research Centre) (2010, November 1), "Helping Moroccan Women Preserve the Argan Tree at the Gateway to the Sahara," https://www.idrc.ca/en/research-in-action/helping-moroccan-women-preserve-argan-tree-gateway-sahara?Publication ID=190

Igrouane, Y. (2017, March 24), "Saad Eddine Othmani: The Journey of a Smiling Islamist," https://www.moroccoworldnews.com/2017/03/211950/saad-eddine-othmani-journey-smiling-islamist/

Inside Arabia (2019, August 18), "#Masaktach: A Movement against Sexual Harassment in Morocco," https://insidearabia.com/masaktach-a-movement-against-sexual-harassment-in-moroc

Jewish Virtual Library (2021), "Jewish Population," https://www.jewishvirtuallibrary.org/jews-of-morocco#1

Kasraoui, S. (2019a, May 15), "New Survey Shows High Rates of Violence against Women in Morocco," https://www.moroccoworldnews.com/2019/05/273120/survey-high-rates-violence-women-morocco/

Kasraoui, S. (2019b, June 28), "Moroccan Port Becomes Largest in Mediterranean with Tanger Med Ii Extension," https://www.moroccoworldnews.com/2019/06/276891/moroccan-port-mediterranean-tanger-med/

Kasraoui, S. (2020, August 27), "European Bank, Moroccan NGO Conclude Loan to Support Women Entrepreneurs," https://www.moroccoworldnews.com/2020/08/316743/european-bank-moroccan-ngo-conclude-loan-to-support-women-entrepreneurs/

Kasraoui, S. (2021, January 6), "Remittances from Moroccan Diaspora Reached $7 Billion in November 2020," https://www.moroccoworldnews.com/2021/01/331151/remittances-from-moroccan-diaspora-reached-7-billion-in-november-2020/

Koundouno, T. F. (2018, July 16), "Morocco has Highest Inequality Index in North Africa: Study," https://www.moroccoworldnews.com/2018/07/250611/morocco-highest-inequality-index-north-africa/

Koundouno, T. F. (2019, August 30), "Report: Expanding Social Disparities, Unequal Wealth Redistribution Killing Morocco's Public Schools," https://www.moroccoworldnews.com/2019/08/281505/report-social-disparities-wealth-redistribution-public-school/

Lovatt, H., and J. Mundy (2021, May 26), "Free To Choose: A New Plan For Peace In Western Sahara," https://ecfr.eu/publication/free-to-choose-a-new-plan-for-peace-in-western-sahara/

McCormick, K. R. (2016, November 29), "She's Challenging Limits to Women's Career Growth in Morocco," https://www.iyfnet.org/blog/shes-challenging-limits-womens-career-growth-morocco

Mebtoul, T. (2020a, February 22), "Morocco to Launch an International Argan Day," https://www.moroccoworldnews.com/2020/02/294372/morocco-to-launch-an-international-argan-day/

Mebtoul, T. (2020b, March 30), "Hashtag Launches Fundraiser for Moroccan Start Ups," https://www.moroccoworldnews.com/2020/03/298057/hashtag-launches-fundraiser-for-moroccan-startups/

Morocco Population 2021 (2021). https://worldpopulationreview.com/countries/morocco-population

Neck, H. M., G. D. Meyer, B. Cohen, and A. C. Corbett (2004), "An Entrepreneurial System View of New Venture Creation," *Journal of Small Business Management* 42(2), pp. 190–208. https://doi.org/10.1111/j.1540-627X.2004.00105.x

Nhairy, S. (2017, December 12), "What Running a Business in Morocco has Taught Me," https://www.entrepreneur.com/article/305953

North Africa Post (2016, October 14), "Proportion of Women in Moroccan Parliament Rises to 21%," https://northafricapost.com/14582-proportion-women-moroccan-parliament-rises-21.html

North Africa Post (2020, February 4), "Morocco Supports SMEs with 'Intelaka' Program," https://northafricapost.com/37630-morocco-supports-smes-with-intelaka-program.html

North Africa Post (2021, March 13), "European Media in Awe of Morocco's Vaccination Campaign," https://northafricapost.com/48235-european-media-in-awe-of-moroccos-vaccination-campaign.html

Renewables Now (2021), "Morocco Opens Call for 400-MWp Noor PV II Project," https://renewablesnow.com/news/morocco-opens-call-for-400-mwp-noor-pv-ii-project-726582/

Rosengren, I. (2020, February 6), "The Women Who Make Argan Oil want Better Pay," https://www.bbc.com/news/business-51370010

Roudies, N. (2010, December 14), "Vision 2020 for Tourism in Morocco," Paper Presented in Trento, Italy. http://www.oecd.org/regional/leed/46761560.pdf

Sang, E. (2018, August 1), "Moroccan Female Entrepreneurs Tackle Misconceptions, Challenges Head On," https://www.moroccoworldnews.com/2018/08/251573/female-entrepreneurs-tackle-misconceptions/

SDGF (Sustainable Development Goals Fund) (2021), "Case Study: Multi-Sectoral Programme for the Fight Against Gender-Based Violence in Morocco," https://www.sdgfund.org/case-study/multi-sectoral-programme-fight-against-gender-based-violence-morocco

Switzerland Global Enterprise (2017, March 29), "Billions of Euros for Morocco's Infrastructure," https://www.s-ge.com/en/article/news/billions-euros-moroccos-infrastructure

Taipei Times (2004, September 24), "Chinese Traders Shake up Moroccan Vendors," http://www.taipeitimes.com/News/worldbiz/archives/2004/09/24/2003204178

Team Weetracker (2018, May 8), "A Guide to Morocco's Start Up Ecosystem," https://weetracker.com/2018/05/08/a-guide-to-moroccos-startup-ecosystem/

Topping, A. (2015), "Counting Women in: Putting Gender Equality at the Heart of Governance in Morocco," https://progress.unwomen.org/en/2015/mohamed/

Toum-Benchekroun, D. (2021, March 14), "Salima El Boussouni's Charming Moroccan Caftans Gain Global Audience," https://www.morocco worldnews.com/2021/03/337315/salima-el-boussounis-charming-moroccan-caftans-gain-global-audience/

Tyson, L. (2021, March 9), "Banque Populaire Launches Microfinance Program for Moroccan Women," https://www.moroccoworldnews.com/2021/03/336901/banque-populaire-launches-microfinance-program-for-moroccan-women/

UN Women (2014, March 27), "Budgets Respond to the Needs of Women in Morocco," https://www.unwomen.org/en/news/stories/2014/3/budgets-respond-to-the-needs-of-women-in-morocco

UN Women (2015, September 17), "In Moroccan Oases Women Watch Plants and Incomes Grow," https://www.unwomen.org/en/news/stories/2015/9/moroccan-oases-women-watch-plants-and-incomes-grow

UN Women (2017, November 14), "Making Stepping out of Home Safer for Women and Girls in Marrakech," https://www.unwomen.org/en/news/stories/2017/11/feature-marrakech-safe-cities

UN Women (2020, July 22), "The COVID-19 Crisis in Morocco Disrupts Value Chains for Women's Cooperatives," https://www.unwomen.org/en/news/stories/2020/7/feature-covid-19-crisis-in-morocco-disrupts-value-chains-for-womens-cooperatives

UN Women (2021), "Moroccan Women Take on Climate Change," https://www.unwomen.org/en/digital-library/videos?id=256c0733-8f6d-4ef0-8a6a-10dcf6f89202

US-Morocco Free Trade Agreement (2021). https://www.trade.gov/us-morocco-free-trade-agreement

Wang, B. Y. (2017), "China 'Going Out' 2.0: Dawn of a New Era for Chinese Investment Abroad," https://www.huffpost.com/entry/china-going-out-20-dawn-o_b_7046790

Wikipedia (2021a), "List of Berber People," https://en.wikipedia.org/wiki/List_of_Berber_people

Wikipedia (2021b), "Rahma el Mouden," https://nl.wikipedia.org/wiki/Rahma_el_Mouden#cite_note-trouw.nl-2

World Bank Group (2021), "Fertility Rate Morocco," https://data.world bank.org/indicator/SP.DYN.TFRT.IN?locations=MA

Worldometer (2021, May 30), "Western Sahara Population," https://www.worldometers.info/world-population/western-sahara-population/

Zahir, G. (2021, February 12), "Moroccan Female Engineering Graduates Outshine European and American Counterparts," https://morocco telegraph.com/education/moroccan-female-engineering-graduates-outshine-european-and-american-counterparts/

© 2022 World Scientific Publishing Company
https://doi.org/10.1142/9789811236600_0003

Chapter 3

Women Entrepreneurs in Algeria

Aidin Salamzadeh
Faculty of Management, University of Tehran, Tehran, Iran

Mirjana Radović-Marković
Institute of Economic Sciencces, Belgarde, Serbia

Boufeldja Ghiat
University of Oran 2, Mohamed Ben Ahmed, Algeria

Abstract

Entrepreneurs play a critical role in the socio-economic development of societies. Among these change agents, women entrepreneurs have drawn the attention of entrepreneurship scholars and policymakers recently. Nevertheless, there is a lack of attention to these entrepreneurs, especially in Arab countries. This chapter reviews the state of Algeria as an Arabic and Berber society. Therefore, after introducing the context, the chapter provides a historical overview of the country. Then, the authors review the main characteristics, motivations, and impacts of the Algerian female entrepreneurs. Afterwards, the gender-specific and constraints to women entrepreneurship in Algeria are discussed and finally, the chapter concludes with some future directions.

Keywords: Algeria, women entrepreneurs, women's entrepreneurship, barriers, motivations, gender

Introduction

As a North African country, the People's Democratic Republic of Algeria (Algeria) is considered the largest Arab and African country. Its neighbours are Tunisia, Libya (to the east), Mali, Niger, and Mauritania (to the south), as well as Morocco (to the west). The country is bounded to the north by the Mediterranean Sea. Due to its geographical characteristics, most of its population live in the northern parts of the country. The surface area of the country is 2,381,741 sq km, and the population is around 44 million, according to the latest approximations as of May 2020 (Boutellis et al., 2021). The official languages of Algerian people are Arabic and Berber; however, majorly, Algerian Arabic is used. In addition, French is used extensively in their education system, governmental writings and media. Thus, their colloquial Arabic is widely affected by French and Berber languages. The majority of the population are Muslims (+97.9%); Christians and Jews are marginalised. As the desert covers the country's southern parts, the weather is warm, especially in the daytime. Then, like several other Arab countries, nights are cool. The coastal parts are rainy, and most of the population live in northern areas rather than the south, which is close to the Sahara Desert.

As one of the emerging economies in the Middle East and North Africa, Algeria has various natural resources, such as oil (16th) and gas (10th) reserves. For many years, the country was and still is among the top ten natural gas exporters worldwide (Abdallah and Khemissi, 2021). Using these resources, Algeria reduced its poverty by up to twenty per cent during the last two decades. This led to maintaining its macroeconomic stability, decreasing its external debt, and increasing its foreign currency reserves (Mokhtara et al., 2019). Nevertheless, Algeria heavily depends on its natural resources, especially oil and gas reserves. Therefore, its economy had experienced tough times when oil and gas prices dropped dramatically in recent years. It was a shock for the Algerian economy and imposed several limitations on the government and the people (Bouraiou et al., 2020; Lebbihiat et al., 2021). Like other oil and gas producing countries, Algeria needs to decrease its dependency on such resources to create a more sustainable economy. Otherwise, global energy market shocks will significantly affect its economy (Settou et al., 2019).

Promoting entrepreneurial activities and liberalisation of the economy are among the two top choices for policymakers to solve this problem (Ghiat, 2019; Sedkaoui, 2019). Nevertheless, the existing trends do not show a significant impact of promoting entrepreneurship on the economic development of Algeria, as the rate and level of entrepreneurial activities are low, and the entrepreneurial ecosystem is not well-developed (Aliouche et al., 2018; Dif et al., 2018). Like many other African countries, the Algerians' and other interested international bodies' social entrepreneurial activities is relatively high. Nevertheless, according to the data released by GEM in 2013, the fear of failure rate was high, and there is a gap between *the will of the State* and *realities on the ground* (Nezai Fatima and Hachemi, 2020).

Besides, like many other Middle Eastern and Arab economies, the role of women in total economic and entrepreneurial activities is marginal (Dana and Dana, 2008; Maaradj, 2009; Nejati et al., 2011; Ghiat, 2014; Setti, 2017). The unemployment rates of women and youth are high, revealing that women are not widely engaged in entrepreneurial activities (Souag and Assaad, 2018). This chapter focuses on elaborating the state of women's entrepreneurship in Algeria. Therefore, in this chapter, after reviewing the historical aspects of the country, which is critical to be studied, the characteristics, motivations, and impacts of the Algerian female entrepreneurs will be scrutinised. Besides, this chapter pays attention to the gender-specific and intersectional constraints to entrepreneurship in Algeria. Finally, the chapter concludes with some remarks on women entrepreneurship in Algeria and some future direction.

Historical Overview

Although the Algerian prehistory, history, language, and Islamic background categorises the country in the Arab world, the Amazigh or Berber population still stick to their valuable cultural heritages[1] (El Aissati, 2005; Aïtel, 2014). Several Amazigh dynasties ruled over this country for centuries until the Ottoman Empire became the ruler (1516–1830) (Ladjal and Bensaid, 2014). They claimed their independence for a short period until France entered into a war with them and governed the country (1830–1962) (Bégué, 1996). Algerians experienced almost three decades of independence until 1991 (Mortimer, 1991). In 1991, the Islamic Salvation Front won the elections, and Algerians afraid of being ruled by an Islamic government cancelled the elections in 1992. It led to shaping civil wars between the elected group and the national armed forces. According to

---

[1] Some passages of the Algerian constitution (preamble and article 4, in pages 1, 3 and 4 of the document) mention this Berber dimension of Algeria, alongside Arabic and Islam. Also, one should consider the Crémieux decree, important because it changed the course of history. The decree imposed French nationality on indigenous Algerian Jews in October 1870, giving them equal rights with the white settlers. Grouping these colonised people with the French colonisers made them look bad and this fueled anti-semitism (see Abitbol & Astro, 1994; Abitbol, 2013).

some estimation, more than one hundred thousand people died due to these wars. The armed Islamic group declared a ceasefire in 1997 (Testas, 2002).

In 1999, a controversial election was held, and the elected president — Abdelaziz Bouteflika — hardly focused on bringing economic stability back to the country. Hopefully, the government took several positive actions, and the country's economic indices improved significantly. Nevertheless, again, the armed Islamic group initiated a war against the government until 2002. The president re-elected in 2004 and 2009, according to the changes made in the constitution (Bouandel, 2009). Several positive actions were considered by the president during his presidency, including improving the economic stability, introducing the Civil Concord initiative, considering a national reconciliation programme, raising the living standards, creating thousands of new jobs, constructing new housings and modernisation of the public sector, which was not working efficiently. In 2019, the elected president — Abdelaziz Bouteflika — resigned after several protests against his intentions to become elected for the fifth time. Therefore, the new president — Abdelkader Bensalah — was elected in 2019. He worked more proactively on socio-economic development plans, citizenship rights, creating political balance, and eliminating corruption; however, many of his actions were condemned by various stakeholders, including activists and journalists (Grewal et al., 2019; Nte, 2021).

Women and Entrepreneurship

Algerian Female Entrepreneurs: Characteristics, Motivations, and Impacts

Women entrepreneurship has become a significant field of research and practice, as female entrepreneurs are changing societies and creating wealth for their nations (Radović-Marković et al., 2012, 2013, 2016). Despite its importance, these entrepreneurs face several challenges to grow, and many of the potential women entrepreneurs could not reach their desired status (Salamzadeh et al., 2019). Although these women entrepreneurs have several common characteristics, motivations and impacts with their men peers, there are several nuances to be considered while studying them, as they face numerous glass ceilings in various societies. This is the same case in Arab countries, in which women are marginalised in terms of Islamic rules and regulations and the customs in these societies (Cheraghi et al., 2014). Nevertheless, not only it does not make these women entrepreneurs reluctant to explore, evaluate, and exploit entrepreneurial opportunities, but it makes them struggle to succeed more proactively (Abadli et al., 2020) (Exhibit 3.1).

Exhibit 3.1 Algerian chef; photograph © Boufeldja Ghiat

Similar to their peers in other societies, the Algerian women entrepreneurs are struggling in two scenes. First, a masculine society that does not believe in their capacities and capabilities (Guillén, 2013), and secondly, going through the valley of death to reach the peak by engaging in entrepreneurial activities (Verhoeff and Menzel, 2011). Like other North African countries (Dana, 2012), as the unemployment rate is high, especially for women and youth, necessity-based entrepreneurship is further developed among Algerian women. Potential women entrepreneurs must have specific characteristics to become entrepreneurs (Welsh et al., 2018). They need to be more ambitious, diligent, resilient, devoted, creative and even taboo breakers (Exhibit 3.2). They must be less conservative, risk-averse, fragile, shy and timid. In addition to their characteristics, their motivations also might be somehow different. They might have various motivations, depending on their background, social class, economic enjoyment, and level of needs. While some are motivated based on economic necessity, others might become entrepreneurs to realise their dreams and gain social respect. Their intentions might be to reach autonomy, become

Exhibit 3.2 Algerian businesswoman; photograph © Boufeldja Ghiat

independent, and emancipate, or to gain equality, eliminate injustice and men's hegemony (Said et al., 2020).

Algerian society knew successive phases of development, from colonialism to independence to economic development. It is highly influenced by traditional culture and knew great socio-cultural changes as a result of globalisation in the late 20th century. The Algerian women were seriously affected by the spread of education and communication technologies, which led to women's emancipation and their motivation to set up their businesses (Ghiat, 2014). The status and social position of the Algerian women went through several eras. They have been characterised by their desire for learning, their insertion in economic activities, and their insertion in entrepreneurship, as shown in Table 1. A different era of development was distinguished by the availability of educational and training opportunities, which impacted women's social position and the nature of professions they occupy.

According to a recent study (Ghiat, 2018), the motivation of women in the Middle East, and especially Algeria, is shaped based on several factors, including (i) economic needs, (ii) insurrection against injustice and male hegemony, (iii) desire for independence and emancipation, (iv) desire for power and respect and (v) self-fulfilment. Nadira (2019) argues that (i) desire for independence, (ii) economic motivations, (iii) job motivations and (iv) family motivations are among the most important motivations for Algerian women entrepreneurs. In another study,

Table 1 Women's social status and occupational developments in Algeria

Women's Struggles	Social status	Nature of work
Struggle for Life	Social backwardness and spread of illiteracy	Work in agriculture or households for the colonists.
Struggle for Social Status	Traditional culture and low-social status	Craft economic activities
Struggle for Economic Insertion	Cultural changes and insertion at work.	Working in female occupations: education, nursing, and secretarial
Struggle for Self -actualisation	Motivation and self-confirmation	Self-employed and small enterprises

Source: authors' elaboration

Mohamed and Hocine (2017) investigated 102 Algerian women entrepreneurs and concluded that personal characteristics — i.e. the search for self-fulfilment, autonomy and independence — are the main motivations of the studied group of entrepreneurs. Interestingly, they argued that 'economic, regulatory and socio-cultural factors have little influence on women entrepreneurial activities'.

In addition to their characteristics and motivations, the impact of women entrepreneurs in their societies is of paramount importance. Most of the existing literature overlooks investigating and measuring the impact of women entrepreneurs in Algeria. Nevertheless, some pieces of evidence have indirectly pointed this out. For instance, some studies implicitly refer to the role of women entrepreneurs in realising social changes in the existing structures of the Algerian society (e.g. Fatima et al., 2014; Ghiat, 2014, Ghiat, 2017; Ghiat, 2018).

Gender-Specific and Constraints to Women Entrepreneurship in Algeria

Despite their lower number compared to men entrepreneurs, women entrepreneurs are key players in developing their societies. These change agents are growing as they find ways to face the existing barriers, especially in male economies. The women entrepreneurs' entry into the entrepreneurship scene of the Algerian economy initiated at the end of the 20th century. Algerian women have become well-educated during the past two decades. Therefore, many intend to establish their businesses. Like most Arab countries, women entrepreneurs suffer from (i) gender inequalities, (ii) traditions and cultural barriers, (iii) religious beliefs, values and norms, (iv) lack of education and networking possibilities, (v) family duties and responsibilities, and (vi) lack of an entrepreneurial culture. Besides, several women entrepreneurs prefer to work informally or add male team members from their family members and relatives. Few of them are supported by various support agencies that offer limited initiatives (Yacine and Djilai, 2021).

Gender inequality has a long history worldwide. The situation is much tricky in Arab countries, where rules and regulations make the gender gap wider than usual (Bastian et al., 2018). Women have recently gained the right to drive and even vote in several Arab countries. The situation in Algeria is much better than the average Arab country's, yet, one could easily witness gender inequality in various interactions, ranging from daily talks to business negotiations (Exhibit 3.3). Algerian women entrepreneurs feel inequality in the process of business venturing as well as their personal lives.

Besides, traditions and cultural barriers are critical issues to be considered (Hattab, 2012). Due to the historical volatilities of Algerians, several traditions and cultural barriers have created for women entrepreneurs. Other significant barriers are the religious beliefs, values and norms, which are primarily rooted in the Islamic traditions in Algeria (Damanhouri, 2017). Religion is an integral part of the Algerian culture and thus could profoundly affect women entrepreneurs' destiny.

Exhibit 3.3 Selling in a bazaar; photograph © Boufeldja Ghiat

In addition to the mentioned barriers, the lack of education and networking possibilities for women entrepreneurs profoundly affects their entrepreneurial activities (Fatima et al., 2014; Radović-Marković and Živanović, 2019). Hopefully, new approaches toward business venturing in the Algerian entrepreneurship ecosystem, such as the emergence of startups and new technology-based firms, augmented this pain recently (Bouguerra, 2015; Doshmanli et al., 2018; Salamzadeh, 2018). During the last two decades, women education and training has improved significantly, and Algerian women are becoming well educated (Exhibit 3.4). Nevertheless, networking possibilities for women are lower than for men, as the male economy has created a glass ceiling for women entrepreneurs. Besides, like women in most countries, women have family duties and responsibilities that could affect their entrepreneurial activities (Ojong et al., 2021). Keeping the balance between work and life has become a significant concern for Algerian women entrepreneurs (Salamzadeh et al., 2014, 2017; St-Jean and Duhamel, 2020). Finally, the lack of an entrepreneurial culture in the Algerian innovation ecosystem makes it harder for [women] entrepreneurs to succeed (Aminova et al., 2020).

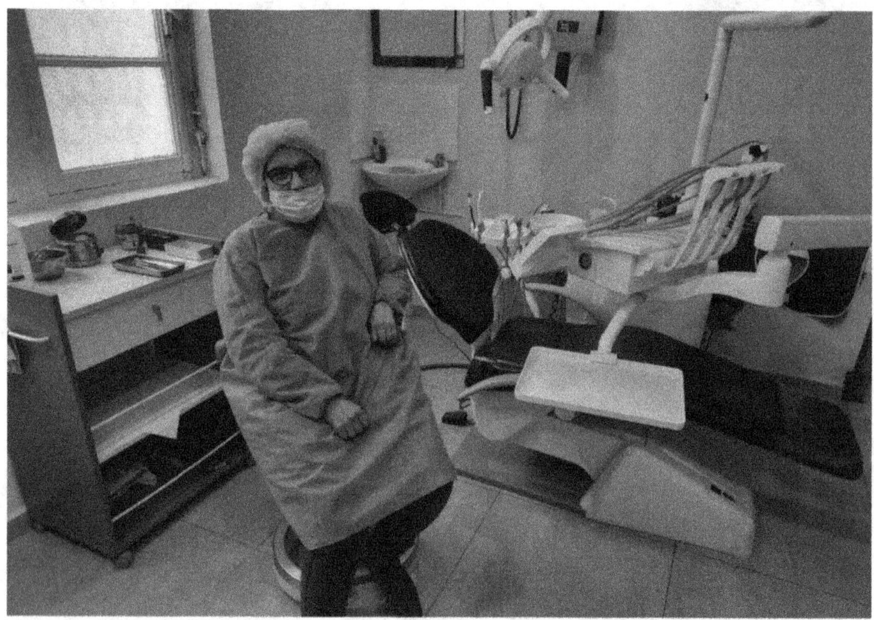

Exhibit 3.4 Female dentist in Algeria; photograph © Boufeldja Ghiat

Toward the Future

According to the World Bank's reports, in 2019, 'Africa has the highest rate of entrepreneurship in the world, and it is the only continent on which women account for the majority of entrepreneurs' (Ojong et al., 2021: 233). Besides, despite several limitations and glass ceilings they face, their contribution to improving innovative activities, creating jobs and wealth, poverty alleviation and enhancing household welfare is significant. The number of researchers who studied the context of women entrepreneurship in Algeria is limited (Ghiat, 2019). Therefore, future researchers might shed more light on the context by making theoretical and practical contributions. Regarding their motivations, characteristics and impacts, several aspects have remained unanswered, especially regarding the impact of women entrepreneurs on the socio-economic development of Algeria and its innovation ecosystems. It is noteworthy that a series of organisations are offering various initiatives to enhance the entrepreneurial activities of Algerian female entrepreneurs. Besides, the nature of female-owned businesses in the Algerian context, including their available resources and relevant strategies to succeed, has remained overlooked.

Then, in terms of managerial and policymaking contributions, it is noteworthy that the Algerian policymakers and government officials must pay sufficient attention to devising relevant policies, providing the required resources and removing barriers for women entrepreneurship (Kabir et al., 2019). Besides, Algerian women entrepreneurs need to know themselves better and take advantage of their potentials, capacities and capabilities. Removing socio-cultural barriers and glass ceilings could be a vital challenge for women entrepreneurs. Then, improving the entrepreneurial culture and enhancing the role of women entrepreneurs in their National Innovation System has become mandatory. As the entrepreneurial ecosystem has evolved dramatically in Algeria during the last years, unleashing the power of women entrepreneurs could make significant changes in Algerian society.

References

Abadli, R., C. Kooli, and A. Otmani (2020), "Entrepreneurial Culture and Promotion of Exporting in Algerian SMEs: Perception, Reality and Challenges," *International Journal of Entrepreneurship and Small Business*, 41(2), pp. 227–240.

Abdallah, H., and G. I. Khemissi (2021), "Macroeconomic Composite Index for Economic Stability: A Kaldorian Analysis for the Algerian Economy," *Dirassat Journal Economic Issue,* 12(1), pp. 697–715.

Abitbol, M. (2013), "The Diverse Reactions to Nazism by Leaders in the Muslim Countries," in A. Meddeb and B. Stora, eds., *A History of Jewish-Muslim Relations,* Princeton: Princeton University Press, pp. 349–374.

Abitbol, M., and A. Astro (1994), "The Integration of North African Jews in France," *Yale French Studies,* 85, pp. 248–261.

Aïtel, F. (2014). *We are Imazighen: The Development of Algerian Berber Identity in Twentieth-Century Literature and Culture,* Florida: University Press of Florida.

Aliouche, E. H., D. B. Fernandez, M. Guechtouli, and W. Guechtouli (2018), "Letting Go of the Oil Addiction: Oil, Entrepreneurship and Franchising in Algeria," *Journal of Management Policy and Practice,* 19(4), pp. 28–34.

Aminova, M., S. Mareef, and C. Machado (2020), "Entrepreneurship Ecosystem in Arab World: The Status Quo, Impediments and the Ways Forward," *International Journal of Business Ethics and Governance,* 3(3), pp. 1–13.

Bastian, B. L., Y. M. Sidani, and Y. El Amine (2018), "Women Entrepreneurship in the Middle East and North Africa," *Gender in Management: An International Journal,* 33(1), pp. 14–29.

Bégué, J. M. (1996), "French Psychiatry in Algeria (1830-1962): From Colonial to Transcultural," *History of Psychiatry,* 7(28), pp. 533–548.

Bouandel, Y (2009), "Algeria's Presidential Election of April 2009: Profile," *Mediterranean Politics,* 14(2), pp. 247–253.

Bouguerra, N. (2015), "An Investigation of Women Entrepreneurship: Motives and Barriers To Business Start Up in the Arab World," *Journal of Women's Entrepreneurship and Education,* 1–2, pp. 86–104.

Bouraiou, A., A. Necaibia, N. Boutasseta, S. Mekhilef, R. Dabou, A. Ziane, et al. (2020), "Status of Renewable Energy Potential and Utilisation in Algeria," *Journal of Cleaner Production,* 246, p. 119011.

Boutellis, A., M. Bellabidi, M. H. Benaissa, Z. Harrat, K. Brahmi, R. Drali, et al. (2021), "New Haplotypes of Trypanosoma Evansi Identified in Dromedary Camels from Algeria," *Acta Parasitologica,* 66(1), pp. 294–302.

Cheraghi, M., Z. Setti, and T. Schøtt (2014), "Growth-Expectations Among Women Entrepreneurs: Embedded in Networks and Culture in

Algeria, Morocco, Tunisia and in Belgium and France," *International Journal of Entrepreneurship and Small Business,* 23(1–2), pp. 191–212.

Damanhouri, A. M. (2017), "Women Entrepreneurship Behind the Veil: Strategies and Challenges in the Kingdom of Saudi Arabia," *Journal of Research in Business, Economics, and Management,* 9(1), pp. 1750–1762.

Dana, L. P. (2012), "Learning from Lagnado About Self–Employment and Entrepreneurship in Egypt," *International Journal of Entrepreneurship and Small Business,* 17(1), pp. 140–153.

Dana, L. P., and T. E. Dana (2008), "Ethnicity and Entrepreneurship in Morocco: A Photo-Ethnographic Study," *International Journal of Business and Globalisation,* 2(3), pp. 209–226.

Dif, A., S. Bourane, and A. Benziane (2018, July), "The Role of the Startup Competition and Entrepreneurial Ecosystem in the Integration of Entrepreneurship Education within the Algerian Universities," in *International Conference on Applied Human Factors and Ergonomics,* Cham: Springer, pp. 140–149.

Doshmanli, M., Y. Salamzadeh, and A. Salamzadeh (2018), "Development of Smes in an Emerging Economy: Does Corporate Social Responsibility Matter?," *International Journal of Management and Enterprise Development,* 17(2), pp. 168–191.

El Aissati, A. (2005), "A Socio-Historical Perspective on the Amazigh (Berber) Cultural Movement in North America," *Afrika Focus,* 18(1/2), pp. 59–72.

Fatima, M., M. El Amine, and H. Khadidja (2014), "Socio-Economic Determinants of Female Entrepreneurship in Algeria," *les cahiers du mecas,* 10(1), pp. 80–90.

Ghiat, B. (2014), "Social Change and Women Entrepreneurship in Algeria," *International Review,* 1–2, pp. 90–100.

Ghiat, B. (2017), "Social Attitudes Toward Women Entrepreneurs in Algeria," *Global Journal of Women Studies,* 1(1), pp. 1–6.

Ghiat, B. (2018), "Understanding Female Motivation for Entrepreneurship in Mena Region: The Case of Algeria," *Socialsci Journal,* 1(2), pp. 136–146.

Ghiat, B. (2019), "Women Managing Men Subordinates in a Males' Society: The Case of Female Entrepreneurs in Algeria," *Open Journal of Women Studies,* 1(2), pp. 35–40.

Grewal, S., M. T. Kilavuz, and R. Kubinec (2019), *Algeria's Uprising: A Survey of Protesters and the Military,* Washington, DC: Brookings Institution.

Guillén, M. F. (2013), "Economic Development, Women Entrepreneurs, and the Future," in M. F. Guillén, ed., *Women Entrepreneurs*, New York: Routledge, pp. 259–280.

Hattab, H. (2012), "Toward Understanding Female Entrepreneurship in Middle Eastern and North African Countries," *Education, Business and Society: Contemporary Middle Eastern Issues*, 5(3), pp. 171–186.

Kabir, M., M. Radović Marković, and D. Radulović (2019), "The Determinants of Income of Rural Women in Bangladesh," *Sustainability*, 11(20), p. 5842.

Ladjal, T., and B. Bensaid (2014), "A Cultural Analysis of Ottoman Algeria (1516–1830) The North-South Mediterranean Progress Gap," *ICR Journal*, 5(4), pp. 567–585.

Lebbihiat, N., A. Atia, M. Arıcı, and N. Meneceur (2021), "Geothermal Energy use in Algeria: A Review on the Current Status Compared to the Worldwide, Utilisation Opportunities and Countermeasures," *Journal of Cleaner Production*, 302, p. 126950.

Maaradj, H. (2009), "Internationalisation of Entrepreneurship in Algeria," *International Journal of Globalisation and Small Business*, 3(3), pp. 239–251.

Mohamed, H., and H. Hocine (2017), "A Multidimensional Analysis of Women Entrepreneurship in Algeria," *Algerian Review of Economic Development*, 6(6), pp. 14–14.

Mokhtara, C., B. Negrou, N. Settou, A. Gouareh, and B. Settou (2019), "Pathways to Plus-Energy Buildings in Algeria: Design Optimisation Method Based on GIS and Multi-Criteria Decision-Making," *Energy Procedia*, 162, pp. 171–180.

Mortimer, R. (1991), "Islam and Multiparty Politics in Algeria," *Middle East Journal*, 45(4), pp. 575–593.

Nadira, B. (2019), "Entrepreneurial Motivation for Algerian Women," *les cahiers du mecas*, 15(2), pp. 95–101.

Nejati, M., Y. Salamzadeh, and A. Salamzadeh (2011), "Ecological Purchase Behaviour: Insights from a Middle Eastern Country," *International Journal of Environment and Sustainable Development*, 10(4), pp. 417–432.

Nezai Fatima, Z., and T. Hachemi (2020), "The Question Of Entrepreneurship in Algeria Between the Will of the State and Realities on the Ground," *Economic Sciences, Management and Commercial Sciences Review*, 13(2), pp. 13–24.

Nte, T. U. (2021), "The Algerian Crisis of 2019 and the Second Arab Spring Uprising: A Comparative Analysis," *International Journal of Public Administration and Management Research,* 6 (2), pp. 16–24.

Ojong, N., A. Simba, and L. P. Dana (2021), "Female Entrepreneurship in Africa: A Review, Trends, and Future Research Directions," *Journal of Business Research,* 132, pp. 233–248.

Radović-Marković, M., C. E. Lindgren, R. Grozdanić, D. Markovic, and A. Salamzadeh (2012), "Freedom, Individuality and Women's Entrepreneurship Education," International Conference — Entrepreneurship Education — A Priority for the Higher Education Institutions, 8–9 October, Romania.

Radović-Marković, M., A. Salamzadeh, and S. M. Razavi (2013), "Women in Business and Leadership: Critiques and Discussions," The 2nd Annual International Conference on Employment, Education, and Entrepreneurship, Belgrade, Serbia.

Radović-Marković, M., A. Salamzadeh, and H. Kawamorita (2016), "Barriers to the Advancement of Women into Leadership Positions: A Cross National Study," International Scientific Conference on Leadership and Organization Development, Kiten, Bulgaria, 16–19 June, 287–294.

Radović-Marković, M., and B. Živanović (2019), "Fostering Green Entrepreneurship and Women's Empowerment through Education and Banks' Investments in Tourism: Evidence from Serbia," *Sustainability,* 11(23), p. 6826.

Said, L., A. Aryati, O. H. Ratnaningrum, and P. Diawati (2020), "Normative, Institutional, and Practical Obstacles in Implementing Women Entrepreneur," *European Journal of Molecular & Clinical Medicine,* 7(11), pp. 1814–1829.

Salamzadeh, A. (2018), "Start-Up Boom in an Emerging Market: A Niche Market Approach," in D. Khajeheian, M. Friedrichsen, and W. Mödinger, eds., *Competitiveness in Emerging Markets,* Cham: Springer, pp. 233–243.

Salamzadeh, A., Z. Arasti, and G.M. Elyasi (2017), "Creation of ICT-Based Social Start-Ups in Iran: A Multiple Case Study," *Journal of Enterprising Culture,* 25(1), pp. 97–122.

Salamzadeh, A., M. Radovic Markovic, and S. M. Masjed (2019), "The Effect of Media Convergence on Exploitation of Entrepreneurial Opportunities," *AD-Minister,* 34(1), pp. 59–76.

Salamzadeh, Y., M. Nejati, and A. Salamzadeh (2014), "Agility Path through Work Values in Knowledge-Based Organisations: A Study of Virtual Universities," *Innovar,* 24(53), pp. 177–186.

Sedkaoui, S. (2019), "An Empirical Analysis of the Algerian Entrepreneurship Ecosystem: Entrepreneurship Ecosystem in Algeria," in S. R. Nair, and J. Manuel Sáiz-Alvarez, eds., *Handbook of Research on Ethics, Entrepreneurship, and Governance in Higher Education,* New York: IGI Global, 476–497.

Setti, Z. (2017), "Entrepreneurial Intentions among Youth in MENA Countries: Effects of Gender, Eeducation, Occupation and Income," *International Journal of Entrepreneurship and Small Business,* 30(3), pp. 308–324.

Settou, B., N. Settou, A. Gouareh, B. Negrou, C. Mokhtara, and D. Messaoudi (2019), "GIS-Based Method for Future Prospect of Energy Supply in Algerian Road Transport Sector Using Solar Roads Technology," *Energy Procedia,* 162, pp. 221–230.

Souag, A., and R. Assaad (2018), "The Impact of the Action Plan for Promoting Employment and Combating Unemployment on Employment Informality in Algeria," *Middle East Development Journal,* 10(2), pp. 272–298.

St-Jean, É., and M. Duhamel (2020), "Employee Work-Life Balance and Work Satisfaction: An Empirical Study of Entrepreneurial Career Transition and Intention Across 70 Different Economies," *Academia Revista Latinoamericana de Administracion,* 33(3/4), pp. 321–335.

Testas, A. (2002), "Political Repression, Democratisation and Civil Conflict in Post-Independence Algeria," *Democratisation,* 9(4), pp. 106–121.

Verhoeff, A., and H. Menzel (2011), "Social Capital to Bridge the Valley of Death, Simulating Critical Incidents in Innovation," *International Journal of Entrepreneurship and Small Business,* 14(1), pp. 149–169.

Welsh, D. H., E. Kaciak, and R. Shamah (2018), "Determinants of Women Entrepreneurs' Firm Performance in a Hostile Environment," *Journal of Business Research,* 88, pp. 481–491.

Yacine, B., & B. Djilai (2021), "Woman Entrepreneurship, Economic Perspectives and Challenges: Case of ANGEM of Mostagnem-Algeria," *Strategy and Development Review,* 11(1), pp. 607–628.

© 2022 World Scientific Publishing Company
https://doi.org/10.1142/9789811236600_0004

Chapter 4

Women Entrepreneurs in Tunisia

Ezzeddine Ben Mohamed
*Faculty of Economics and Management, University of Sfax, Tunisia and College of
Business and Economics, Qassim University, Saudi Arabia*

Lassaad Makhlouf
Faculty of Economics and Management, University of Sfax, Tunisia

Research Unit CODECI - University of Sfax - Tunisia

Elhem Ben Fatma
*Faculty of Economics and Management, University of Sfax, Tunisia and College of
Business and Economics, Qassim University, Saudi Arabia*

Amina Omrane (Corresponding author)
*Faculty of Economics and Management, University of Sfax, Tunisia ECSTRA
Research Centre, IHEC-Carthage, Tunisia*

Abstract

Entrepreneurship is a major driver of development, especially in developing countries such as the countries of North Africa. In this chapter, we will study women entrepreneurship in Tunisia. We have tried to paint a fair picture of the main transformations that the Tunisian economy and society have witnessed, starting with the end of French colonialism. We also discussed the evolution of the concept of female entrepreneurship in Tunisia and reviewed the most important elements of the support given to entrepreneurs and the extent of its suitability, especially for businesswomen. Finally, the future of women entrepreneurship in Tunisia was discussed.

Keywords: Tunisia, women entrepreneurship, economic and social transformations, entrepreneurial success.

Introduction

According to Mohamed Talbi in the *Encyclopaedia Britannica*, the Republic of Tunisia (with one legislative house, the Assembly of People's Representatives᾽ including 217 members) is the northernmost country and the smallest nation in North Africa. It is located in the Maghreb region, and it is bounded by Algeria to the west and southwest, by Libya to the southeast, and by the Mediterranean Sea to the north and east. It covers a total area of 163,610 km^2 (involving the African conjunction of the western and eastern parts of the Mediterranean Basin), with a population of 11,870,000 million (in 2020) (of which 68.9% is urban and 31.1% rural).

Tunisia's accessible Mediterranean Sea coastline and strategic location have attracted conquerors and visitors throughout the ages, and its ready access to the Sahara Desert brought its people into contact with the inhabitants of the African interior. After achieving independence in 1956, Tunisia targeted to modernise and flourish its economy with a transformative social agenda. However, as Tunisia remained an authoritarian state where citizens were suffering from oppressive regimes, lack of freedom and democracy, and a low standard of living, anti-government protests and armed rebellions were spread across the country, leading to spring Tunisia's Jasmine Revolution political and social changes in 2011. Currently, Tunisia is considered as the only fully democratic state in the Arab World in the Economist Intelligence Unit's Democracy Index, with one of the highest per capita incomes in the continent.

Arabic is the official spoken language in Tunisia, and most natives speak a dialect of Tunisian Arabic. However, it seems that actually a tiny fraction of the population installed in the south (in Taoujout for instance), still speak one of the Berber languages (i.e., Amazigh). French, introduced during the protectorate continues to be used in the press, education and government. To a lesser extent, English also serves as the third teached language.

Like many other African countries, Tunisia has been suffering from many economic and political problems, which began since the Arab spring revolution in 2011 (Ben-Slimane, Justo, and Khelil, 2020). Indeed, as its unemployment rate is becoming higher attaining more than 30% for female university graduates, the government has been seeking to promote entrepreneurship by encouraging adults and young graduates to launch their own projects. Many programmes and development plans have been also dedicated in order to support such initiatives. Nevertheless, the major observation to retain is that women role and their participation to the economic growth has remained weak compared to those of men. In fact, it was argued in many recent reports, such as the Arab Barometer Report (Robbins and Thomas, 2018), that women are still encountering some problems and facing many challenges (cultural, psychological, financial and institutional ones) whenever they decide to develop new ventures. Fortunately, many of them have been successful and struggled enough to yield successful companies and start-up. Their activities emerge and are triggered by the interplay between political, economic, social and cultural contexts (Ojong et al., 2020).

This chapter intends to analyse and provide an in-depth understanding of the situation of Tunisian women entrepreneurs. For this purpose, after presenting an historical overview of the country, the main drivers, motives and difficulties faced by women entrepreneurs will be outlined. Moreover, a specific attention will be drawn on the governmental support structures and their role in promoting the entrepreneurial culture among women. Finally, the chapter concludes by suggesting some future orientations.

Historical Overview

Tunisia has a very rich history. From early antiquity, Tunisia was inhabited by the indigenous Berbers. The Romans occupied Tunisia for almost 800 years, after defeating Carthage in 146 BC, introducing Christianity and leaving architectural legacies like the amphitheatre of El Jem.

Julius (2018) noted that Jews preceded Arabs in Djerba by 1,000 years. After several attempts starting in 647 BC, Muslims conquered Tunisia by 697, bringing Islam and the Arab culture to the local inhabitants. In 1574, the Ottoman Empire established a control on Tunisia and held sway for over 300 years, until the French conquered it in 1881.

With the proclamation of independence in 1956, the country did not have a great economic asset: less productive agricultural land, less developed port infrastructure, narrow internal market, low savings, high unemployment and embryonic industrial equipment. The annual growth rate of 4.7% from 1950 to 1954 even fell to 2.8% until 1960. The priority was then to free the national economy from French control, which had favoured agriculture and mineral extraction but had largely neglected industry, Tunisia then being the least industrialised country in the Maghreb. Between 1956 and 1960, the aim of the authorities was public control in key sectors, such as rail and air transport, banking, electricity and other infrastructure. The government nationalised, between 1959 and 1960, the large companies which were under French control. The aim was to fortify the control of the new independent state while maintaining a liberal policy based on the promotion of investment and foreign trade. Thus, during the first five years, the state offers tax incentives and credit facilities in order to motivate the private sector to play a more important role.

In 1961, political leaders opted for this new strategy and expanded state control over all areas of the economy. The principal objectives are 'economic decolonization', improving the standard of living of the population, reducing dependence on external capital (and therefore greater self-sufficiency) and creating a national market. This phase is witness to an acceleration of the collectivization process, in particular in the agricultural sector. Following the expropriation of land in foreign possession in 1964, France froze all financial help to Tunisia, thus plunging the country into a serious economic crisis. In 1969, Tunisia signed a first trade agreement with the EEC, thus easing the repercussions of the crisis. However, the collectivization rate had then reached 90% in the agricultural sector; the public sector includes wholesale and retail trade, a significant part of industry and the banking sector and transport, electricity and mines that were already under state control. Only the tourism sector, which the authorities are developing, escapes entirely state management. The cooperatives will however be maintained until March 1970 and the movement will have generated a series of industrial creations and launched the establishment of tourist activity.

From 1970 Tunisia is shifting to a market economy and private property. The new government then encourages a retreat of the state of the industrial sector by opening it to private investment. It is also creating new institutions whose purpose is to promote the private sector, such as the Agency for the promotion of industry, with the aim to streamline, modernise and simplify the industrial policy.

During the 1970s, Tunisia experienced an expansion of the private sector and a rapid development of manufacturing employment. The country is thus recording an average growth of 8.4% per year and the per capita income goes from 314 to 1,351 dollars. However, the structure of industrialisation was characteris market economy is less decisive than announced: Tunisia largely maintains the subsidisation of certain prices, the financial sector is entirely managed by the government, and the economy is protected by very high customs duties and import restrictions. The public sector remains dominant but is declining, with a gradual dissociation between sectors open to external competition and those intended for the internal market. This opening allows the creation of jobs, the development of better social mobility of newly educated youth, and the growth of a middle class.

The decline in oil revenues, the external debt, the growing deficit in public finances, the absence of a sufficient productive base to absorb the surplus labour force, and the lack of State investment in infrastructure, are the major events that marked the beginning of the 1980s (Morisson and Talbi, 1996).

This is why the Sixth Development Plan (beginning in 1982) was designed to introduce the necessary economic adjustments to prepare Tunisia for a period marked by declining oil revenues. The investment is mainly directed toward the non-oil industries. In addition, external debt and the balance of payments are tightly controlled, the public investment was reduced and the consumption submitted to restrictive measures through a wage freeze and additional import restrictions. However, most of the plan's objectives are not successful: GDP growth remains below 3%, the current account deficit stands at 7.8% of GDP and the external debt stands at 56% of GDP.

In 1986, Tunisia experienced its first year of negative growth since independence. The government officially agrees with the International Monetary Fund (IMF) on the establishment of a structural adjustment programme (SAP) by signing an agreement on an 18-month economic recovery programme. In 1988, Tunisia was granted recourse to extended funds for three years. Subsequently, the loan period was extended several times until 1992, demonstrating the confidence of the organisation in the government's ability to implement a structural reform of the economy. The principal aim of the SAP is the total or partial transfer of certain public services for the benefit of banks or private groups.

The programme strategy is implemented in the seventhand eighth development plans. It aims to achieve macroeconomic stability and introduce the initial measures of structural liberalisation while reducing dependence on oil exports. The results are not stable due to the vulnerability of agriculture and the effects of the Gulf War. Nevertheless, the plan can be considered successful: the major internal and external imbalances are under control, the external debt remains reasonable and GDP growth of 4.3% on average is achieved. The main purpose of the following plan is to increase efficiency and promote market mechanisms.

The government has privatised state-owned enterprises to put an end to their indebtedness. It started by privatising small and medium-sized beneficiary enterprises. The sectors concerned are above all tourism, construction materials, textiles, the food industry and fishing, mechanics and electrical engineering. Ratifying the GATT agreements in 1990 then joining the World Trade Organisation in 1995, Tunisia must then develop the competitiveness of its products and improve its comparative advantages, in order to have freer access to international markets, by adopting an overall economy upgrade programme. In addition, an association agreement signed with the European Union in July 1995 led from 1996 to the gradual dismantling of customs barriers until January 1, 2008. In addition, the government encouraged the manufacturing industry to produce only for export by giving it the possibility of establishing itself anywhere in the country while working under regulating free trade zones. These economic reforms are now shown as an example by international financial institutions.

The process of globalisation, which affects Tunisia, is conceived as a 'natural order', that is to say that it is obligatory for the country in order to avoid a strong deterioration of its economic situation. The policy of openness has allowed a lasting resumption of economic growth, but at the same time contributed to the modification of the economic fabric. The Tunisian economy is thus divided into two sectors: a competitive sector and a sector weakened by a process of opening to which they have not prepared, especially in the strategic textile sector, which represented nearly 50% of exports in 2004. The nature of this upgrading process enabled the Tunisian State to retain a significant capacity for intervention and to develop new sectors including that of the mechanical industry and new technologies. It is about focusing on quality and making the most of the advantage of Europe's geographical and cultural proximity.

This upgrading policy has led to a modernisation of production techniques and business management procedures and encouraged foreign direct investment. However, it has not significantly increased productive investment and job creation. In addition, a report of the World Bank dated June 2004 had pinned the 'discretionary interventions of the government' and the 'power of the insiders' which weakened, according to it, the business climate and risk-taking of foreign investors. The bad debts of Tunisian public banks, which could explain the moderate level of foreign investment reinforced this phenomenon. In this context, the private sector is still mainly made up of small and medium-sized family enterprises (SMEs) which, according to the National Institute of Statistics, contributed 72% of the GDP in 2006; they accounted for 85% of exports and 56% of the total volume of investments.

Moreover, persistent unemployment and the difficulties linked to the slow restructuring of the State leave part of the population on the margins of economic development, which is the principal basis of the government policy.

In 2011, the nepotism of the family of the former president and the problem of corruption (feeling of inequality in society, disparities between regions, lack of freedom, unemployment in interior regions, ...), played an important role in the triggering of the Tunisian Jasmine Revolution. We can cite the Jemna oasis experience which refers to moral challenges that Tunisians sought through advocating to values of solidarity, dignity and freedom (Ben Slimane et al., 2020).

Therefore, after the Arab Spring (characterised by similar anti-governmental resistance movements in Egypt and Libya), the economy has been drooping but then recovered with 2.81% GDP growth in 2014. Tunisia's political and social transition gained a new momentum in early 2014, with the adoption of a new constitution and the appointment of a new government. This consensus will allow for further reform in the economy as well as the public sector; however, the terrorists attacks of 2015 led to the collapse of, not only the tourism but also all the Tunisia's economy (Ben Jelili, 2016).

Women and Entrepreneurship

Women entrepreneurship in Tunisia is one of the dimensions of the Tunisian development plan. The Tunisian government has worked since independence to consolidate the role of women and make them effective partners in development.

During the French colonial period, Tunisian women and their families worked on the farms of the French colonialists, and for long years after independence, Tunisian women worked in small farms and raised livestock and poultry as small enterprises. The main purpose of these projects was to provide the basic requirements for the families of these women.

Women entrepreneurship in this period was mainly related to the agricultural sector. Almost all families, especially rural ones, depended on the role of women and their success in managing these primitive activities to achieve the basic necessities of life. Women entrepreneurship also appeared in Tunisia at an early age, as the state, especially in the 1980s, encouraged the creation of small projects in the textile industry, such as the traditional carpet (Organisation Internationale de Travail, 2016). In many Tunisian cities such as Kairouan, Tunis, Gabes or Sfaqis, many Arab traditional souks were established in order to promote such hand-made traditional products and handicrafts (Exhibits 4.1 and 4.2).

Exhibit 4.1 El Medina bazaar, Tunis; photograph © Ayoub Tarchoun

As supported by Zelekha and Dana (2019), in more than 50 African countries, cultural capital has a significant influence on the tendency to develop entrepreneurial projects, even in a low-trustworthy environment with a nonsupportive social capital. Fortunately, in some other North African countries like Tunisia, it has been argued that entrepreneurs' social capital, raised via the development of their social skills, has an overall

Exhibit 4.2 El Medina ElArbi souq, Sfax; photograph © Amina Omrane

significant impact on their access to external resources (financing, strategic information), an then on their success, especially in the High-technology field (Omrane, 2013, 2014, 2015). Indeed, in Tunisia where the majority of women entrepreneurs are Muslim, it seems that religiosity has no significant effect on female entrepreneurs' performance. However, the concept of *wasta*, which is an Arabic concept that having personal connections with influential others/stakeholders is a critical key to women's success in their business venturing (Baranik et al., 2018).

Despite the main effects of networking on Tunisian women willingness to develop their own projects, it seems that the majority of them insist on establishing their own companies in order to be independent and to assume their own responsibilities, to get better profits, to afford sufficient incomes for their family duties, or in some cases to continue developing their family businesses (CREDIF, 2020) as for women motives worldwide (Ramadani et al, 2017). We can cite many illustrative examples of Tunisian successful family female-led companies specialised in pastry goods and cakes, such us *Gourmandise,* founded in 1967 by Mrs Radhia Kammoun (Exhibit 4.3), or *Masmoudi,* created in 1972 by Mrs Moufida Masmoudi.

Exhibit 4.3 Radhia Kamoun, founder of Gourmandise; photograph ©
Amina Omrane

Female entrepreneurship in Tunisia is an increased phenomenon. In fact, according to the official government statistics, two thirds of higher education graduates were women. However, their participation rate in the labour force is only 26% compared to 70% for men. In the other hand, 75% of working women get paid. The number of female entrepreneurs heading the 'legal entity' type of business is 19%. The presence of women in corporate boards does not exceed 5.3% and only 23% of the businesses are headed by female entrepreneurs. When it comes to wages, Tunisia is ranked 37th globally in terms of gender pay equity (specifically for rural women who are suffering from weak pension and low pay) and loans' women beneficiaries represent 43%, with only 29% of the total amounts provided by the Tunisian Bank of Solidarity (TBS). As for the Palestinian National Office for the Middle East, the share of women in loans granted is 9% of the beneficiaries with an average loan of 158 thousand dinars compared to 232 thousand dinars for men.

Therefore, through the results shown above, it is noteworthy that in such an unfavourable Tunisian labour market, women are not enjoying economic and social rights equal to men, even if the Personal Status Code (promulgated by Habib Bourguiba in 1956) has allowed their emancipation. Indeed, under the provisions of this code, Tunisian women have the right to be well educated as well as to get an important place in society, compared to other women in the Arab world (Murphy, 1999). However, several cultural and social stereotypes remain present as their chances of getting fair employment, similar salaries, governmental support and promotion at work, are being jeopardised, weakening their skills and believes in their potentialities (Ouanes, 2016). On the other hand, in a population where the third of young university graduates suffer from unemployment, the best solution for recent graduates, especially for female ones, is to pave the way for the development of entrepreneurial projects and the establishment of new ventures, despite the difficulties and obstacles they may encounter. This fact may explain to what extend necessity entrepreneurship exceeds voluntarist entrepreneurial activities in high-unemployment countries (Dana, 2012). Similarly, El Harbi et al. (2009) pointed out that in less-developed countries, the majority of female entrepreneurs develop necessity enterprises. In such cases, women may have been pushed into entrepreneurial activities to escape from unemployment. In some other cases, many contextual factors and cultural inhibitions may affect negatively their decision to create their own firms, such as autocracy, bureaucracy, as well as the existence of entrepreneurial milieus, which as located in urban specific regions, and not in others (Touzani et al., 2015). For instance, in many Tunisian interior and rural regions, the entrepreneurial ecosystem seems so restricted that farmer women, who constitute the backbone of agricultural work (especially during the olive picking season), remain poorly paid despite their hard efforts, and do rarely think about developing their own farms (Exhibit 4.4).

Main Challenges Faced by Women Entrepreneurs in Tunisia

In developing countries, especially those pertaining to the African continent but also in many other emergent nations like India, women are facing many challenges and problems that impede and inhibit their intention and desire to be entrepreneurial (Agarwal et al., 2021). In this regard, the prior literature emphasised that the main obstacles experienced by women entrepreneurs whenever they decide to enact ventures revolve around access to finance and liquidity, legal issues, restricted access to business networks, cultural barriers, as well as lack support offered by administrations and public centres (Halkias et al., 2011). In fact, more than 60% of Tunisian women entrepreneurs get the financial resources required for their ventures either from their own savings, or via the love money they obtain from their families, friends and/or relatives (CREDIF, 2020). In addition, women have usually multiple roles

Exhibit 4.4 On the farm; photograph © Amina Omrane

to assume such as family household chores, children care, especially in a masculine society which does not encourage her enough to develop her leadership skills or to hold decision-making positions of responsibility (Robbins and Thomas, 2018).

That is why many researchers have recommended the necessity of opening up new entrepreneurial opportunities for women in order to enable them to go beyond gender disparity and grow up successful projects (Carter et al., 2015; Cited by Agarwal et al., 2021). However, it appears that necessity entrepreneurs are not ultimately the most unsuccessful ones. We can notice how much young Tunisians, especially those with high university degrees, have been struggling those last years to seek help from other successful Arab entrepreneurial experiences, and to launch and develop startups, as it is the case in Dubai, in the United Arab Emirate or in Egypt. We can cite *Dabchy (online platform of women dressing),* as a newly start-up owned by the young inspiring entrepreneur Mrs Ameni Mansouri in 2016 (Exhibit 4.5).

Governmental Support Dedicated for Women Entrepreneurs

The Tunisian government has enacted the 'Start-Up Act', legislation that helps reduce the barriers faced by young entrepreneurs, where bureaucracy and administrative and legal difficulties are most stated by owners.

On this optic, it is noteworthy to highlight also the effective role of business accelerators that are making their way in Tunisia. We can cite 'Intilaq', which is the first accelerator founded in Tunisia in 2014. It aims at contributing, with Flat6Labs, to support, guide and even finance the ideas for new projects and startups in various fields, including services, multimedia, and high technology.

In another perspective, different types of structures and support programmes intervene in the process of business creation (public or private support structures, non-governmental organisations, national and international support programmes, etc.). These structures provide information, support and advice to promoters to enable them to materialise and develop their businesses. The many existing support structures are dispatched throughout the country and offer their free services to entrepreneurs in terms of specialised training, support, personal coaching and technical assistance, facilitation of business start-up procedures and finally follow-up projects. Most of these structures are attached to the ministries of industry, agriculture, employability and trade.

The Industry and Innovation Promotion Agency (APII): A public establishment whose mission is to implement the Tunisian government policy relating to the promotion of the industrial sector. The APII offers a wide range of services in the form of information, support, assistance,

Exhibit 4.5 Ameni Mansouri, startupper and CEO of "Dabchy.com" photograph ©
Amina Omrane

partnership, studies while ensuring the granting and management of benefits.

The National Network of Business Incubators: This network is led by the APII under the aegis of the Ministry of Industry. This network offers several services. They are:

- Information relating to the environment for the creation of businesses in Tunisia and to the industrial fabric.
- Managerial and entrepreneurial training.
- Incubation: These are personalised assistance sessions for the validation of the project idea, the realisation of the business plan as well as support in the search for financing and the creation of businesses.
- Accommodation: This allows the promoter to set up his innovative business in the premises of business incubators under advantageous pricing conditions. During the hosting, the promoter benefits from logistical services (office equipment, fax, internet, etc.) as well as the expertize available.

The Agricultural Investment Promotion Agency (APIA): This government agency's main mission is to promote private investment in the fields of agriculture, fisheries and related services. It provides services for granting financial and tax advantages to promoters of agricultural and fishing projects. This structure also allows the identification of investment opportunities and project ideas as well as the assistance of young agricultural promoters and their supervision during the implementation phase of their projects through training and the development of project studies.

Business centres offer developers and investors the services necessary for the launch or development of their projects. These centres also provide support to promoters in the start-up and monitoring phases of their projects.

The National Office of Tunisian Handicrafts (ONA): This company implements the State's strategy in terms of safeguarding and developing the Tunisian craft sector, in particular the promotion of investment and support to the creation of employment, innovation and creativity and the development of policies for the preservation of artisanal heritage.

The Export Promotion Centre (CEPEX): This structure works to increase the export of Tunisian products and services with high added value while strengthening the positioning of Tunisian products and services internationally.

In addition to state structures, post-revolutionary Tunisia is marked by an associative, active and dynamic fabric. According to statistics from the government presidency, there are 1,826 associations working in the field of sustainable development and in particular entrepreneurship. The areas on which these associations are working are multiple and lie at the centre of the entrepreneurial value chain starting with information and entrepreneurial culture through to post-creation monitoring and support.

Among the key actors, we can cite in this non-exhaustive list: UTICA, CONECT, IACE, Réseau Entreprendre, Mercy Corps, INJAZ, Enpact, Wajjahni, Scouts, CEED, CJD, Tunisian Ambassadors for Development, ONUDI, Mazam, Souk Tanmia, WES, Intilaq, Switchmed, Lab'ess, TCSE.

These organisations or support centres for new entrepreneurs have played and still play an important role in the development of the spirit of initiative and help to facilitate the accessibility of information with simplified guides in order to encourage young people to turn their dreams into realities. However, promoters in several regions are unable to cooperate with this associative fabric due to a lack of information on the very existence of these centres.

Toward the Future

Entrepreneurship is a decisive tool for giving young people the opportunity to guarantee their financial autonomy and to integrate into economic life by creating wealth and added value.

To develop a real entrepreneurial culture within the various communities, the involvement of school remains essential, if not indispensable. The Tunisian entrepreneurial context is promising. However, the major drawback of that context lies in the education system. This system does not respond to the new orientations of young people which become more entrepreneurial. Several studies show the lack of adequate entrepreneurship education at Tunisian schools, unlike that which is in developed countries (OECD, 2012). The promotional efforts of Entrepreneurship in primary and secondary education remain modest.

For the higher education, it is evident that universities around the world are assuming new responsibilities not only by becoming an important engine of economic development but also by becoming more involved in the teaching of strategic and functional skills related to entrepreneurship.

In Tunisia, entrepreneurial education has been launched for more than a decade through specific lessons scheduled at universities. Despite the shortcomings observed, positive results can be seen from these educational programmes:

- Entrepreneurial culture courses have increased students' interest in starting a business.
- New entrepreneurs were assisted in the development of their business ideas.
- Various actions aim to develop skills and integrate students into their environment entrepreneurship.

Weaknesses include the lack of an elite programme for graduates who start their own businesses or the lack of tools and appropriate educational resources. Likewise, the courses are very heterogeneous and often unsuitable. It is therefore necessary to find a better balance between theory / practice in the design of courses and the type of professional/teacher speaker through better collaboration between university institutions and support structures Universities should provide education including awareness of entrepreneurship, promotion of technology transfer and knowledge and commercialization of research results.

The other component of the education system which plays a fundamental role in entrepreneurship is vocational training following a training course is a source of entrepreneurial inspiration. The intention to start one's own business arises when the entrepreneur opts for training. Thus, national efforts have been made to better adapt the legislative framework relating to the development of vocational training programmes. On a technical, educational and organisational level, the entrepreneurial training experiences have enabled learners to improve their entrepreneurial skills in several regions of the country. The vocational training system in Tunisia despite the efforts made did not promote more entrepreneurship. To do this, it is useful to:

- Establish a national strategy for the development of the entrepreneurial spirit including the various stakeholders.
- Provide training centres with the necessary resources and the appropriate mode of operation to train in entrepreneurship.
- Train trainers more on entrepreneurship pedagogy.
- Pay particular attention to risk taking,
- Support learners interested in entrepreneurship.

In view of the previous observations on women entrepreneurship, it appears that it becomes more than necessary to implement an exhaustive support programme for the integration of the entrepreneurial culture beyond the vocational training centres. The government has set up entrepreneurship training programmes for young graduates through public and private institutional support, in order to compensate for the lack of experience and skills to successfully carry out entrepreneurial activities. These programmes are geared toward developing an 'entrepreneurial profile' with the personal and technical skills required by new projects. However, they remain not sufficient to motivate young graduates and to encourage them to build up successful ventures. It is also recommended to develop a more cohesive entrepreneurial ecosystem with an adequate infrastructure, which enables adults, wherever they are, to create easily their own projects.

In another perspective, in order to shorten the gender gap in entrepreneurship, the government is conveyed to facilitate the access to financing and liquidity for women. Associations and non-governmental organisations could also play an important role, not only in fighting against social and cultural masculinity stereotypes, but also in promoting female success and women empowerment for a better economic development (Omrane and Bag, 2020).

References

Agarwal, S., Ramadani, V., Dana, L.-P., Agrawal, V. and Dixit, J.K. (2021), "Assessment of the significance of factors affecting the growth of women entrepreneurs: study based on experience categorization", *Journal of Entrepreneurship in Emerging Economies*, Vol. ahead-of-print No. ahead-of-print. https://doi.org/10.1108/JEEE-08-2020-0313

Baranik, L. E., B. Gorman, and W. J. Wales (2018), "What Makes Muslim Women Entrepreneurs Successful? A Field Study Examining Religiosity and Social Capital in Tunisia," *Sex Roles* 78, pp. 208–219. https://doi.org/10.1007/s11199-017-0790-7

Ben Jelili, R. (2016), *Les Reformes Economiques en Tunisie: Une Urgence en Quête de Leadership*, Tunis: Sud Editions, 248p.

Ben Slimane, K., R. Justo, and K. Khelil (2020), "Institutional Entrepreneurship in a Contested Commons: Insights from Struggles Over the Oasis of Jemna in Tunisia," *Journal of Business Ethics* 166(4), pp. 673–690.

Carter, C., S. Mwaura, M. Ram, K. Trehan, and T. Jones, (2015). "Barriers to Ethnic Minority and Women's Enterprise: Existing Evidence, Policy Tensions and Unsettled questions," *International Small Business Journal: Researching Entrepreneurship*, 33(1), pp. 49–69. https://doi.org/10.1177/0266242614556823

Centre de recherches, d'études, de documentation et d'information sur la femme (CREDIF) (2020), http://www.credif.org.tn

Dana. L. P. (2012), "Learning from Lagnado about Self–Employment and Entrepreneurship in Egypt," *International Journal of Entrepreneurship and Small Business* 17(1), pp. 140–153.

El Harbi, S., A. Anderson, and N. Mansour (2009), "The Attractiveness of Entrepreneurship for Females and Males in a Developing Arab Muslim Country: Entrepreneurial Intentions in Tunisia," *International Business Research* 2(3), pp. 47–53.

Halkias, D., C. Nwajiuba, N. Harkiolakis, and S. M. Caracatsanis (2011), "Challenges Facing Women Entrepreneurs in Nigeria," *Management Research Review* 34(2), pp. 221–235.

Julius, L. (2018), *Uprooted: How 3000 Years of Jewish Civilisation in the Arab World Vanished Overnight*, Portland, Oregon: Vallentine Mitchell.

Morisson C., and B. Talbi (1996), *La Croissance de l'Economie Tunisienne en Longue Période.* Paris: OECD.

Murphy, E. (1999), *Economic and Political Changes in Tunisia: From Bourguiba to Ben Ali*, London. Macmillan Press.

OECD (2012), "Promouvoir l'Entrepreuneuriat dans les Universités Tunisiennes," Etudes sur les Qualifications et les Compétences en Entreupreunariat en Tunisie, Report prepared by the LEED/OECD program, 114 pages.

Ojong.N., A. Simba, and L. P. Dana (2020), "Female Entrepreneurship in Africa: A Review, Trends, and Future Research Directions," *Journal of Business Research* 132, pp. 233–248.

Omrane, A. (2013), "Les réseaux sociaux de l'entrepreneur et son accès aux ressources externes: le rôle des compétences sociales (The entrepreneur's social networks and his access to external resources: The role of social skills)," *Management et Avenir*, 65, pp. 73–93.

Omrane, A. (2014), "Social Determinants of Seed-Stage Entrepreneurs' Success in the High-Technology Field," *International Journal of Business Environment*, 6(4), pp. 373–394.

Omrane, A. (2015), "Entrepreneurs' Social Skills and Access to External Resources: The Role of Social Capital," *International Journal of Entrepreneurship and Small Business,* 24(3), pp. 357–382.

Omrane, A., and S. Bag (2020), "Which Effective Linkages between Women Empowerment and Economic Development in India," *International Journal of Business Excellence. Forthcoming Issue,* 20 pages.

Organisation Internationale du Travail (2016), "Evaluation Nationale du Développement de l'Entreupreunariat feminin en Tunisie ILODWT for North Africa and ILO country Offices for Egypt and Eriterea," 130p. https://www.ilo.org/wcmsp5/groups/public/---ed_emp/---emp_ent/---ifp_seed/documents/publication/wcms_551170.pdf

Ouanes, M. H. (2016), "Entrepreuneuriat en Tunisie: Recommandations pour Relever les Defis Economiques," C A Perspectives on Tunisia N°03. Center for Applied Policy Researsh.

Ramadani.V., L. P. Dana, N. Sadiku-Dushi, V. Ratten, and D. H. B. Welsh (2017, December), "Decision-Making Challenges of Women Entrepreneurship in Family Business Succession Process," *Journal of Enterprising Culture* 25(4), pp. 411–439.

Robbins, M., and K. Thomas (2018), "Women in the Middle East and North Africa: A Divide Between Rights and Roles," Arab Barometer–Wave IV Topic Report, 16, https://www.arabbarometer.org/wp-content/uploads/AB_WomenFinal-version05122018.pdf.

Touzani, M., F. Jlassi, M. A. Adnan, and R. Bel Haj Hassine (2015), "Contextual and Cultural Determinants of Entrepreneurship in Pre- and Post-Revolutionary Tunisia: Analysing the Discourse of Young Potential and Actual Entrepreneur. *Journal of Small Business and Enterprise Development,* 22(1), pp. 160–179.

Zelekha, Y., and L. P. Dana (2019), "Social Capital Versus Cultural Capital. Determinants of Entrepreneurship: An Empirical Study of the African Continent. *The Journal of Entrepreneurship,* 28(2), pp. 250–269. https://doi.org/10.1177/0971355719851900.

© 2022 World Scientific Publishing Company
https://doi.org/10.1142/9789811236600_0005

Chapter 5

Women Entrepreneurs in Libya

Saurabh (Mobi) Singh
Kent State University, Kent, Ohio, USA

Robert Hisrich
Kent State University, Kent, Ohio, USA

Abstract

The ability to successfully engage in entrepreneurship is contingent on numerous factors including societal norms, overall market environment and economic conditions in which entrepreneurs operate. The topic of female entrepreneurs has attracted much attention during the past few decades. It is an interesting phenomenon as it tests the general assumptions among people about the perceived characteristics of entrepreneurs and possible impact of gender differences in outcome of entrepreneurial activities. This chapter provides insights about the unique societal and economic conditions in Libya and how these affect women entrepreneurs. The chapter also discusses potential strategies for female entrepreneurs that might be utilised to appropriately collect rent from entrepreneurial opportunities in Libya.

Keywords: Libya Economy, Female Entrepreneurs, Opportunities, Entrepreneurial Strategies.

Introduction

Entrepreneurship is the activity of generating and appropriating rent from opportunities. Entrepreneurs differ from other people based on their capabilities to create, discover and exploit opportunities. Furthermore, entrepreneurs are not homogeneous; it has been shown that context/

environment can affect the identification of opportunities for entrepreneurship (Dana, 1995).

Ojong et al. (2021) review the extant scholarship on female entrepreneurs in Africa, taking stock of relevant resources, strategies and contexts; this chapter focuses on women entrepreneurs in the North African country of Libya.

According to a 2021 survey published by Statita.com, Libya has a population of 6.3 million and is the 17th largest country in the world by land area. The same survey emphasised the fact that big metropolitan areas such as Tripoli account for 90% of country's population; with Islam being the self-reported religion of 97% of the population. The gross domestic product of the country has declined from its peak in 2012 at around 80 billion to a present level of 33 billion US dollars. The author of the survey reported that oil production accounted for 80% of gross domestic product making up a total of 97% of country's exports. Without doubt, crude oil production and export is primarily the main industry in the country leaving room for growth in other industries.

The country has a very high rate of unemployment with unemployment numbers rising from 18% in 2019 to a whopping 19.4% in 2020 (O'Neill, 2021). Extremely high level of unemployment is not surprise as the phenomenon might be correlated with underdevelopment of numerous industries other than those related to oil production and exports. Coupled with unemployment crisis, Libya is facing an ongoing political crisis. Based on an overview of Libya published by World Bank in 2021, the country is facing a governance competition between militant and political groups. The overview from World Bank emphasised that the Libyan National Army (LNA) and Government of National Accord (GNA) control different regions of the country in a competing fashion. Based on the same overview, the LNA and GNA have agreed to parliamentary elections in December 2021; however, the impact of political turmoil on economy of Libya might be witnessed for years to come.

Entrepreneurial opportunities are instances when entrepreneurs might be able to introduce new products, services or raw materials and be able to generate wealth by selling them at prices higher than the cost of production (Casson, 1982). Opportunities might be a result of external shocks to existing markets, which might be discovered by potential entrepreneurs (Shane, 2003). Another possibility is that the opportunities are created by entrepreneurs with a desire to generate and appropriate rent (Alvarez and Barney, 2004). Regardless of the fact whether opportunity is created or discovered, the concept of opportunity relies on the assumption that there are competitive imperfections in the markets (Venkataraman, 1997). Entrepreneurs might be able to generate wealth for themselves when competitive imperfections exist, and they can capitalise on them (Alvarez and Barney, 2004). Such competitive imperfections might be entry barriers, variation in the level of information and capabilities among potential entrepreneurs, transaction costs, and so on (Alvarez and Barney, 2004). In the case of Libya, the list of number and types of competitive imperfections is beyond comprehension. The country is in the middle of political and economic crisis, which might enable some entrepreneurs to successfully capitalise on competitive imperfections created by the instability in Libya.

The probability of an entrepreneur discovering opportunity depends on whether they have access to necessary information related to discovering the opportunity before other entrepreneurs can, whether the concerned entrepreneur has the cognitive abilities to process the information and realise the utility of the opportunity (Kirzner, 1973). The differences in the level of knowledge among entrepreneurs in Libya might be higher than other nations because of the higher levels of economic and political uncertainty in the country. High levels of uncertainty might influence entrepreneurial decisions of people who might have access to information about opportunities (Gaglio and Katz, 2001). Potential entrepreneurs differ in terms of their willingness to bear risk created by uncertainty, which might also influence entrepreneurial intentions among people who have information about opportunities (Douglas and Shepherd, 2000). Entrepreneurial opportunities might be abundant in Libya, but potential entrepreneurs might not be willing to bear risks of uncertain political and economic environment in the country.

One of the key benefits that drive entrepreneurs toward opportunities is the possibility of generating rent for themselves. An entrepreneur who can successfully generate and capture rent for themselves must have the necessary knowledge and resources to capitalise on the opportunity, and the entrepreneurs must have ability to appropriate the rents for themselves and not for other entrepreneurs (Alvarez and Barney, 2004). The rent generation and appropriation process is called Arbitrage and might be facilitated by creating a formal governance mechanism such as a start-up or an entrepreneurial firm (Alvarez and Barney, 2004). Potential entrepreneurs in Libya might face multiple issues in rent arbitrage. First, they might not have access to ample resources to capitalise on the opportunity. Second, they might have issues appropriating rents for themselves as the evolving economic and political environment might hamper such capabilities.

The behaviour of entrepreneurs depends on the 'rules of the game'. Rules of the game are the reward structures of the economy, which vary over decades or centuries and are contingent on the social, political and economic environment, which the entrepreneur operates in (Baumol, 1990). Libya is currently facing an economic and political turmoil that might have significant impact on the rules of game, and the reward structures available to entrepreneurs might be different from other countries. In such instances, entrepreneurial efforts might be allocated to productive or non-productive tasks, which might in turn help or hurt the economy (Baumol, 1990).

Historical Overview

Indigenous Amazigh people have been in the region of Libya since time immemorial. Jews lived here from the time of Greek rule during the 3rd century BC until the 20th century. Islam arrived here during the 7th century AD. In 1510, Spain occupied Tripoli.

From 1551 to 1912, all of today's Libya was Ottoman Tripolitania. From 1912 to 1927, this was Italian North Africa (see Exhibit 5.1). As of 1927, it was ruled as two separate Italian colonies, Italian Cyrenaica surrounding Benghazi and Italian Tripolitania around Tripoli. In 1934, the name Libya was adopted. Rossetto (2021) discussed the sense of Italian identity that existed here from the 1920 until the 1960s.

In September 1940, the Italian invasion of Egypt was launched from Libya. During the 1942 Battle of El Alamein, British forces defeated the Nazis, resulting in British occupation. Exhibit 5.2 features a British Middle East Forces (MEF) postage stamp used in Benghazi in September 1944.

Women and Entrepreneurship

Female entrepreneurship is a growing trend in Libya. The country has witnessed turbulence in terms political and economic stability, which might in turn make fulfilment of entrepreneurial dreams even harder for female entrepreneurs. Although there is no definitive marker, there is a chance that the Libyan society might be male dominated. The claim might find support from the fact that only 15.96% of seats in national parliament are held by women; women find themselves impacted by unemployment as the employment-to-population ratio for females above 15 years of age is only 25.8% (USAID IDEA, 2021). The numbers are alarming for the outlook of

Exhibit 5.1 Map of the Italian Empire; photograph © Léo-Paul Dana

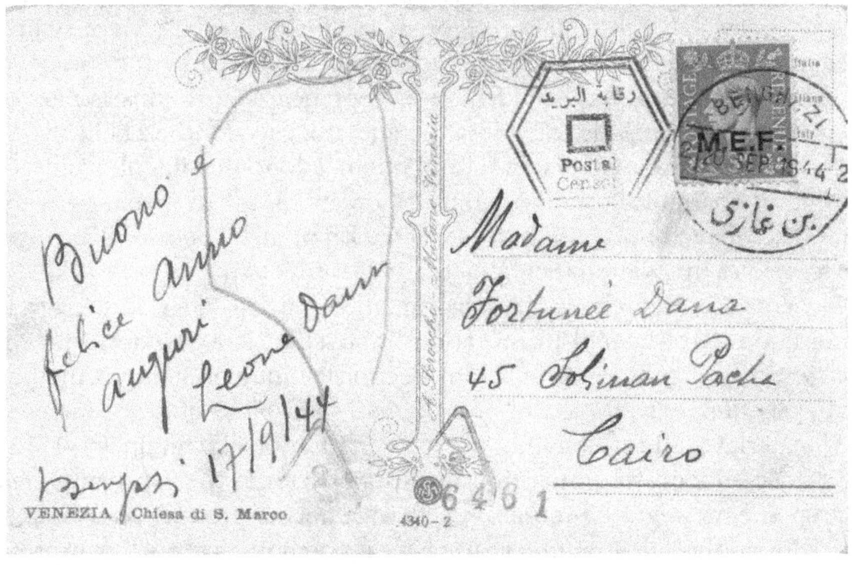

Exhibit 5.2 Postcard with British stamp used to mail it from Libya to Egypt; photograph © Léo-Paul Dana

female entrepreneurship, but it might not be the end of tunnel. Exhibit 5.3 depicts a scene from a bazaar; the image is a representation of male dominance in business world in North African countries as store owners are predominantly male.

In this section, we will discuss the strategies that female entrepreneurs in Libya might utilise to benefit successful realisation of their entrepreneurial goals. Although the economic and political environment of Libya has a lot of uncertainty, there might be some unique opportunities created by such environments. Female entrepreneurs might be able to generate and appropriate rent for themselves by creating new entrepreneurial ventures. In general, intentionality, resources, boundaries and exchange are essential properties of an organisation (McKelvey, 1980: 115). The goals of entrepreneurs shape the intentionality of a new venture (Van De Ven, 1980), whereas resources might be physical, financial, or human and intellectual capital (Vesper, 1980). Boundary is the demarcation between the venture and its environment (Katz and Kahn, 1978). Exchange is the number of frequency of transactions with other entities outside the boundary of the venture (Katz and Kahn, 1978). All the properties are critical for female entrepreneurs in Libya. First, the intentionality of entrepreneurial ventures founded by females in Libya might be heavily influenced by gender stereotypes and uncertainty in political and economic environment. The resources available to female entrepreneurs might also be extremely limited in Libya. Such factors might shape ventures formed by entrepreneurs in Libya in a critical ways and female entrepreneurs must utilise strategies to maximise opportunity capitalisation and arbitrage for their benefit.

Female entrepreneurs in Libya might adopt the intentionality of invention or innovation. Entrepreneurs might engage in invention when they discover an opportunity, and exploitation of such opportunities might be termed as innovation (Schumpeter, 1934).

Female entrepreneurs in Libya might be more likely to engage in innovation as compared to invention. Innovation is associated with the following: new good or service introduction, unique or alternate method of production, exploitation of new market, availability of new sources of raw materials and formation of unique organisations (Schumpeter, 1912). Higher likelihood for innovation finds support from the fact that female entrepreneurs might be more likely to introduce a product or service to market that their male counterparts have ignored in past. Such new products or services might meet unmet needs of specific target populations and be created from unique sources, which might have been underutilised

Exhibit 5.3 Dominance of men is evident in Libya; photograph courtesy of www.pexels.com

by male entrepreneurs. The unique resources might be human capital in such as skilled labour or arts artistic skills that females in Libya might have traditionally engaged in. Additionally, the novel products or services introduced in market by female entrepreneurs might meet the needs of consumers in other countries with similar demographics, socio-political and economic environment leading to opening of new markets.

Female entrepreneurs might also be able to enhance success probabilities of opportunity seeking and exploitation by the formation of unique firms such as organic firms. Organic firms in general have the characteristics of having informal culture with information being symmetrically distributed across people associated within the organisation (Lumpkin and Dess, 1996). Organic firms are more suitable for environments that are evolving and have high levels of uncertainty; adapt to changing consumer needs in a highly efficient way (Miller, 1983). Female entrepreneurs in Libya might face a political and economic environment that is extremely uncertain, and the needs of consumers might also be ever evolving. Utilising an organic organisation structure for their new venture firms might enable them to convert the challenges created by uncertainty into potential competitive advantages. Female entrepreneurs might also benefit from unique organic structures as most industries in Libya are underdeveloped besides the ones related to crude oil production and export. The adoption of organic structure might help them capture the benefits of environmental munificence. Environmental munificence is the overall growth and profit probability of an industry (Lumpkin and Dess, 1996). It is beyond doubt that environmental munificence for products or services originating from female owned entrepreneurial ventures in Libya is high because the political and economic environment in the country might stabilise in future.

Females with a desire to capitalise on opportunities in Libya might face a big hurdle of lack of resources. Under such circumstances, it is ideal for them to adopt the strategy of bricolage. Bricolage is creating something useful from whatever is available as resource to achieve the objective (Miner et. al., 2001). Certain entrepreneurs might utilise worthless resources, which might hold no face value to other entrepreneurs in terms of usefulness, to capture opportunities (Baker and Nelson, 2005). It is also possible that female entrepreneurs might utilise constructive radicalness to successfully achieve their entrepreneurial objectives. Radicalness is the characteristic of innovativeness of entrepreneurs where they do not follow existing norms and try very new means of achieving their innovation objectives (Hage, 1980, Kimberly, 1981). Female entrepreneurs in Libya

Exhibit 5.4 Women in Libya; photograph courtesy of www.pexels.com

need to adopt a radical approach toward implementing innovativeness in their entrepreneurial ventures to overcome the barriers preventing the realisation of their innovative objectives.

To be a successful entrepreneur, potential female entrepreneurs in Libya must equip themselves with entrepreneurial orientation. Entrepreneurial orientation is 'processes, practices, and decision-making activities that lead to new entry' (Lumpkin and Dess, 1996). Autonomy, innovativeness, risk taking, proactiveness and competitive aggressiveness are five dimensions of entrepreneurial orientation (Lumpkin and Dess, 1996). Female entrepreneurs in Libya must realise that in a possibly male-dominated society like Libya, it is useful to assert autonomy. Autonomy might help the potential female entrepreneurs to break the barriers preventing them from taking first steps toward creating an entrepreneurial venture. Female entrepreneurs must also be willing to take risks even the economic and political environment is highly uncertain. Proactiveness is the degree to which people differ in terms of their current actions toward future problems or changes (Collegiate Dictionary, 1991: 937). Female entrepreneurs might be competing with exiting male or female entrepreneurs in the market, and a competitive aggressiveness is a must for them to succeed. Competitive aggressiveness is the entrepreneur's attitude toward taking actions, which might challenge industry rivals and support growth of endogenous ventures (Lumpkin and Dess, 1996).

Toward the Future

The cause of supporting female entrepreneurs has drawn attention from numerous international agencies such as the United Nations Development Programme (UNDP), the European Union and the Euro-Mediterranean Women's Foundation. The UNDP supports the UNDP Libya unit which has received funding from the European Union to establish the Tatweer Entrepreneurship Development Campus (TEC) (UNDP, 2021). Based on the UNDP website, the TEC has an objective to support an environment for entrepreneurial growth in Libya.

The contest drew entrepreneurial ideas from entrepreneurs, and the objective of the contest was to support an environment for entrepreneurial growth as well as promote peace and economic stability in Libya. The UNDP also supports the cause of mental health of female entrepreneurs and in accord with that objective, it helped establish Mental Health and

Psycho-Social Support Centre in Tommina, which provides psychological and social support to female entrepreneurs. Through the centre, UNDP hopes to achieve the objective of lowering gender inequalities in Libyan economy. Exhibit 5.4 is a representation of female attire in North Africa. Women are expected to dress up in attire driving barriers to gender equality even higher.

The European Union has funded other programmes such as Support to Libya for Economic Integration, Diversification and Sustainable Development (SLEiDSE), which has an objective to diversify entrepreneurial gender makeup of Libyan economy and empower women (Libya Business News, 2019).

References

Alvarez, S., and J. Barney (2004), "Organizing Rent Generation and Appropriation: Toward a Theory of the Entrepreneurial Firm," *Journal of Business Venturing* 19, pp. 621–635.

Baker, T., and R. Nelson (2005), "Creating Something from Nothing: Resource Construction through Entrepreneurial Bricolage," *Administrative Science Quarterly* 50, pp. 329–366.

Baumol, W. (1990), "Entrepreneurship: Productive, Unproductive, and Destructive," *Journal of Political Economy* 98, pp. 893–921.

Casson, M. (1982), *The Entrepreneur,* Totowa, NJ: Barnes & Noble Books.

Dana, L.-P. (1995), "Entrepreneurship in a Remote Sub-Arctic Community: Nome, Alaska," *Entrepreneurship: Theory & Practice,* 20(1, Fall), pp. 55–72. Reprinted in Norris Krueger, Ed., *Entrepreneurship: Critical Perspectives on Business and Management,* Volume IV, London: Routledge, 2002, pp. 255–275.

Douglas, E., and D. A. Shepherd (2000), "Entrepreneurship as a Utility Maximizing Response," *Journal of Business Venturing* 15, pp. 393–410.

Gaglio, C. M., and J. Katz (2001). "The Psychological Basis of Opportunity Identification: Entrepreneurial Alertness." *Journal of Small Business Economics* 12(2), pp. 95–111.

Hage, J. (1980), *Theories of Organizations,* New York, NY: Wiley.

Katz, D., and R. L. Kahn (1978), *The Social Psychology of Organizations,* New York, NY: Wiley.

Kimberly, J. R. (1981), "Managerial Innovation," in P. C. Nystrom and W. H. Starbuck, eds., *Handbook of Organizational Design,* Vol. 1, 84–104. New York, NY: Oxford University Press.

Kirzner, I. M. (1973). *Competition and Entrepreneurship,* Chicago: University of Chicago Press.

Libya Business News. (2019). "EU Helping Young and Women Entrepreneurs in Libya," https://libya-businessnews.com/2019/08/28/eu-helping-young-and-women-entrepreneurs-in-libya/

Lumpkin, G., and G. G. Dess (1996), "Clarifying the Entrepreneurial Orientation Construct and Linking it to Performance," *Academy of Management Review* 21, pp. 135–172.

McKelvey, B. (1980), *Organizational Systematics,* Berkeley, CA: University of California Press.

Miller, D. J. (1983), "The Correlates of Entrepreneurship in Three Types of Firms," *Management Science* 29, pp. 770–791.

Miner, A. S., P. Bassoff, and C. Moorman (2001), "Organizational Improvisation and Learning: A Field Study," *Administrative Science Quarterly* 46, pp. 304–337.

Ojong, N., A. Simba, and L.-P. Dana (2021), "Female Entrepreneurship in Africa: A Review, Trends, and Future Research Directions," *Journal of Business Research* 132, pp. 233–248.

O'Neill (2021), "Libya–Unemployment Rate 1999–2020 | Statista," https://www.statista.com/statistics/808770/unemployment-rate-in-libya/

Rossetto, P. (2021), "'We Were all Italian!': The Construction of a 'Sense of Italianness' Among Jews from Libya (1920s–1960s)," *History and Anthropology,* https://doi.org/10.1080/02757206.2020.1848821, https://kfunigraz.academia.edu/PieraRossetto/CurriculumVitae

Schumpeter, J. A. (1912), *The Theory of Economic Development, Leipzig: Duncker and Humblot.* English ed. Cambridge, MA: Harvard University Press, 1934.

Schumpeter, J. A. (1934), *The Theory of Economic Development,* Cambridge, MA: Harvard University Press.

Shane, S. (2003), *A General Theory of Entrepreneurship: The Individual–Opportunity Nexus,.* Northampton, MA: Edward Elgar.

UNDP (2021), "Women Leaders at the Heart of Sustainable Development in Libya | UNDP in Libya," https://www.ly.undp.org/content/libya/en/home/presscenter/articles/2018/Women-leaders-at-the-heart-of-sustainable-development-in-Libya.html

USAID IDEA (2021), "Country Profile: Libya," https://idea.usaid.gov/cd/libya/

Van de Ven, A. H. (1980), "Early Planning, Implementation, and Performance of New Organizations," in J. R. Kimberly and R. H. Miles, eds., *The Organization life cycle,* San Francisco, CA: Jossey-Bass, pp. 83–134.

Venkataraman, S. (1997), "The Distinctive Domain of Entrepreneurship Research: An Editor's Perspective," in J. Katz, and R. Brockhaus, eds., *Advances in Entrepreneurship, Firm Emergence, and Growth,* Vol. 3., Greenwich, CT: JAI Press, pp. 119–138.

Vesper, K. H. (1980), *New venture strategies,* Englewood Cliffs, NJ: Prentice-Hall.

Webster's ninth new collegiate dictionary (1991), Springfield, MA: Merriam Webster.

World Bank (2021), "The World Bank in Libya," [online] https://www.wor ldbank.org/en/country/libya/overview

© 2022 World Scientific Publishing Company
https://doi.org/10.1142/9789811236600_0006

Chapter 6

Women Entrepreneurs in Egypt

Hadia Fakhr El Din
The British University in Egypt, Cairo

Christine Samy
Leeds Trinity University, UK

Rania Miniesy
The British University in Egypt, Cairo

Abstract

This chapter examines the constraints and opportunities for female entrepreneurs in Egypt. It describes the context in Egypt through general evidence about unemployment in the country and sheds light on the current reforms taking place to support women. It provides a historical overview on female entrepreneurship and explains how some factors bear on female entrepreneurship in Egypt. The authors build on this to establish how digital technology can provide the means to female entrepreneurs to overcome the constrictive challenges and barriers faced in Egypt. Within the remit of this chapter, the aim is to expound the role of social media in supporting Egyptian women entrepreneurs. It is projected that the findings from this study will have practical and policy implications for enhancing female entrepreneurial participation and supporting it in Egypt.

Keywords: female entrepreneurs, Egypt, social media, ICT

Introduction

Egypt is an important geopolitical and economic player in the Middle East and North Africa (MENA). This is rooted for several reasons. First, its economy is one of the most diversified economies in the region (IMF, 2020) with manufacturing (Exhibit 6.1), hydrocarbons, and tourism (Exhibit 6.2) as well as a thriving agriculture sector that supplies plenty of healthy food to the Egyptian people (see Exhibits 6.3 and 6.4). Second, its geopolitical position, lying in the crossroad of three continents and two seas; the Suez Canal (Exhibit 6.5) is an important asset. Third, Egypt is one of the most populated countries in Africa with a population that reached 103.3 million in January 2021 (World Bank, 2021). This last point, however, brings several challenges that hinder its socio-economic development, like low levels of education, and inadequate health conditions. One major issue raising serious concerns in Egypt is the high unemployment among women and youth (Constant et al., 2020). Many people are pushed to self-employment as a means to survive (Exhibit 6.6).

The roots of high unemployment rates in Egypt can be traced to the1950s when the educational system was restructured by President Gamal Abdel Nasser. Nasser introduced free education for all Egyptian citizens to fight the high illiteracy rates at the time and assured that all

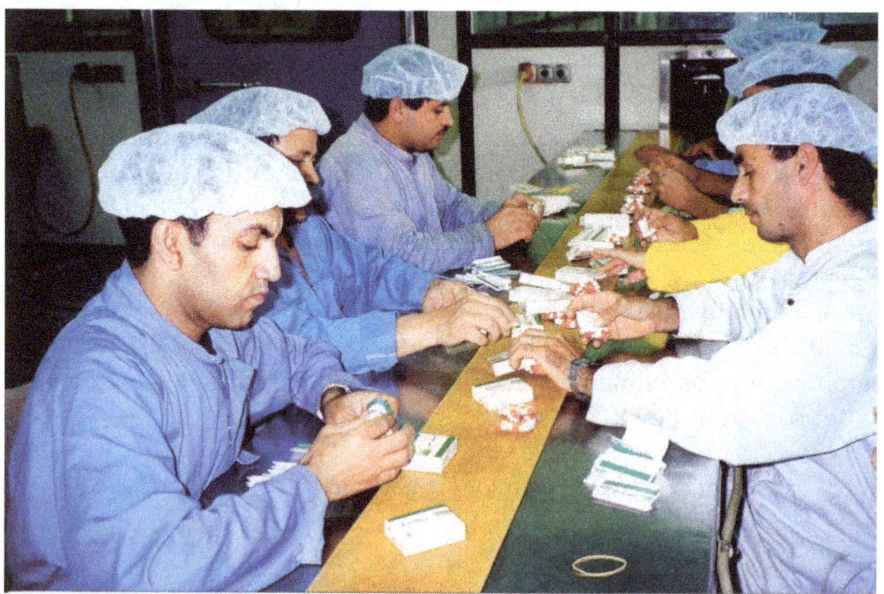

Exhibit 6.1 Pharmaceutical factory; photograph © Léo-Paul Dana

Exhibit 6.2 The Great Sphinx of Giza; photograph © Léo-Paul Dana

Exhibit 6.3 Fresh watermelon delivery; photograph © Léo-Paul Dana

Exhibit 6.4 Fresh tomatoes for sale; photograph © Léo-Paul Dana

Exhibit 6.5 Suez Canal at Port Fouad; photograph © Léo-Paul Dana

Exhibit 6.6 Subsistence shoe-shiners in Cairo; photograph © Léo-Paul Dana

university graduates would be employed in the public sector (Loveluck, 2012). However, not long after, the government was unable to absorb the vast numbers of graduates into the public sector, especially after President Sadat (1970–1981) reduced the criteria of admission to Egyptian Universities and established new universities all over Egypt, which multiplied the number of graduates (Ghafar, 2016). Moreover, in 1974, Sadat (in power 1970–1981) introduced an Open-Door Economic Policy (ODEP) or as widely known *infitāh,* which stimulated the country's private sector and encouraged a laissez-faire (Dana, 1993) approach. Yet, it also resulted in surfacing the country's economic inequalities (Exhibit 6.7) and growth in the rate of unemployment. Accordingly, later during the Mubarak era (1981–2011), the public and the private sectors were incapable of generating enough jobs in the country and the neoliberal reforms had negative consequences, which contributed to the 2011 uprising (ILO, 2011).

Following the political unrest of 2011 and its consequent economic challenges, the government took robust actions resulting in an era of key economic reforms in the country, which had an impact on entrepreneurs

Exhibit 6.7 Some with cars and others with a donkey-cart; photograph © Léo-Paul Dana

in general and more specifically on female entrepreneurs. The increase in the entrepreneurial activity in Egypt resulted in Cairo (Exhibit 6.8) being featured in Forbes' list of top cities starting new ventures (Guttman, 2015).

Notwithstanding the low level of Egyptian women's economic participation, there is a significant progress that has been made in the execution of Egypt's long-term vision, echoed in Egypt's 2030 Development Strategy (OECD, 2018). In addition, a National Strategy for Women has been advanced by the National Council for Women (NCW), which launched the first National Strategy for Women's Empowerment in 2017. The NCW Women Strategy embraces four main aspects including political empowerment, economic empowerment, social empowerment and protection against all forms of violence (NCW, 2017). The general plan is to focus on reducing female unemployment and growing female formal labour participation. Although female entrepreneurship is growing, still men are leading in this field in the MENA region according to recent reports (GEM, 2021).

In this book chapter, we provide a historical perspective on the development of female entrepreneurship in Egypt. We carried out a survey of the literature of female entrepreneurship in Egypt to shed a particular focus on the Egyptian context while relating it to an overview of female

Exhibit 6.8 El Tahrir Square, formerly Ismailia Square, in Cairo;
photograph © Léo-Paul Dana

entrepreneurship in the region. We then portray the different challenges
and barriers faced by these women based on recently published reports.
Finally, this chapter endeavours to show how social media (SM) and information and communication technologies (ICTs) provide a timely solution
to face these challenges and overcome the barriers in the pursuit to support
and enhance female entrepreneurship in Egypt.

Historical Overview

Egyptian women have always played entrepreneurial roles throughout the
years, particularly if we look through the wider definition of the term. They
have exhibited various entrepreneurial traits, such as finding new possibilities, thinking creatively, and taking risks. Despite the strong patriarchal
traits and traditional restrictions, Egyptian women challenged their society
and plunged into different businesses usually dominated by men.

Women entrepreneurship in Egypt has complex roots and historical
investigations of the Egyptian society point to many women figures who
ran businesses and made a career in different industries, which can be
traced back to as early as the ancient Egyptians.

According to Van Heel (2015), Egypt has had female entrepreneurs since the ancient days, where pictures — on tomb walls and on papyrus papers — of ancient Egyptian women who had strong control over their own lives and were leading work themselves were common. An example is Tsenhor — a choachyte or a funerary service provider (Exhibit 6.9). Tsenhor was born around 550 BC in South Egypt and according to evidence used to bring offerings to the departed and was supported by her husband (Van Heel, 2015). The papyri reflected her extensive entrepreneurial traits

Exhibit 6.9 Ancient Egyptian woman in front of an offering table; public domain photograph

and showed that she was an entrepreneur in her own right who enjoyed a degree of financial independence, bought land, and owned houses. Tsenhor expanded the family business and continued the funerary services business of her father (Van Heel, 2015).

According to several historians, the first decades of the 20th century were vivacious for women in Egypt (Cormack, 2021). They created new economic and social possibilities in various fields and domains. For instance, in the entertainment industry, visionary female entrepreneurs dominated the Egyptian scene during the post-World War II years. According to Danielson (1991) during this era, Egyptian women's activities extended into all areas of commercial entertainment and its management. Similarly, in culture, women founded several magazines and periodicals. A strong relevant example is Fatma al Youssef (Exhibit 6.10), who founded a

Exhibit 6.10 Fatma El Youssef; public domain photograph

magazine in her name in 1925, which is published until today. Fatma (Rose) al-Youssef — originally an actress of Levantine origins — was known for her determination and was considered a patron of the Arab female press who managed to renew the intellectual scene in Egypt.

Another example is Aziza Amir (Exhibit 6.11), the godmother of Egyptian cinema (Fertat, 2016), who is often labelled as the founder of the cinematic art in Egypt (Farrugia, 2002). It is said that she gave birth to the Egyptian long feature film by taking the risk of producing the very first long movie in Egypt. She played a significant role in the history of Egyptian cinema for her innovative cinematic themes between the 1920s and the 1950s (Farrugia, 2002).

Egypt also had pioneering female social entrepreneurs who had a desire to empower other women. For example, Hidiya Afifi Barakat established in 1919 a significant grassroots society *Société de la Femme Nouvelle* (New Woman Society) to focus on setting up schools for girls in the neglected countryside (Exhibit 6.12).

Exhibit 6.11 Aziza Amir; public domain photograph

Exhibit 6.12 Countryside enterprise; photograph © Léo-Paul Dana

Varying in their scope and aims, what the above examples have in common is a degree of innovation, an extent of risk (Drucker, 1970; Knight, 1921) and the creation of new social and economic opportunities, which provides a very relevant description of entrepreneurship and of what these females were adding to their communities and the Egyptian society.

Women and Entrepreneurship

As entrepreneurship is vital for economic growth, employment and innovation (Farzanegan, 2014), it is of strategic importance in developing countries. Alkasmi et al. (2018) suggested that the MENA region has become a thriving hub of entrepreneurship and is demonstrating unceasing growth due to the size of the region, its young population (Exhibit 6.13) as well as its increased access to technology. Women entrepreneurship is of high importance in this region, as it can enhance the national economies of these countries, reduce poverty and contribute to gender equality (Beninger et al., 2016). Thus, it is not surprising that there have been increasing and serious attempts by governments and other stakeholders to support and enhance the well-being and development of women in the region. This covers economic, social and political aspects that seek to improve their conditions/lives. Accordingly, countries in the area have been/are adopting programmes and policies focusing on the societal engagement, empowerment and emancipation of their women citizens. However, there is still scarce literature on the development of women entrepreneurship in the region (Beninger et al., 2016), as well as in its individual countries.

Exhibit 6.13 Young and enthusiastic; photograph © Léo-Paul Dana

Women comprise around half of the Egyptian population but represent no more than 18% of its labour force (World Bank, 2019). They face considerable challenges in the labour market, which are generally attributed to the adverse social, economic and regulatory environments (ElAshmawy, 2016). In the GEM 2017 report, evidence suggests that there is a noteworthy increase in both the percentage of women entrepreneurs, from 16% to 29%, and the percentage of female established business owners, from 7% to 20% (Ismail et al., 2017). However, the lowest rates of female entrepreneurship are still reported in Egypt, with gender gaps of about 70% (Elam, 2019). Moreover, the same report (2019) highlights that females have a lower probability of continuance in comparison to men-led businesses. Although there are improvements in the levels of female entrepreneurship, the last GEM report shows that there are more than two male entrepreneurs for every female entrepreneur in Egypt (GEM, 2021), and female unemployment is four times as much as that of men (CAPMAS, 2020).

Womenfolk have been confronted with many challenges compared to men (Dana, 2012). As is the case in other countries in North Africa, Egyptian women entrepreneurs face various obstacles: gender disparity (GEM, 2021), limited knowledge of markets (Adam et al., 2017), lack of access to technology, no access to business networks and limited capital and financial services (UNIDO, 2018). Traditionally, apprentices have been men (Exhibit 6.14) while women lacked business skills and capacity building (Mahrous, 2019).

Exhibit 6.14 Learning the blacksmith trade; photograph © Léo-Paul Dana

In addition, it is not always culturally welcomed for females to engage in business (Dana, 2000). According to El Mahdi (2020), women face more difficulties when hiring workers, setting up the business and in marketing and they sometimes even encounter harassment and are they challenged by aggressive competition in the market. Moreover, social norms still locate the family care burden and household chores solely on women's shoulders, even if they work (ElShorbagi et al., 2017). This prohibits women from gaining experience and from creating their own social networks, which later hinders their ability to successfully establish and run an enterprise (ElShorbagi et al., 2017).

Ojong et al. (2021) examined trends of women entrepreneurs across Africa. In Egypt, as elsewhere, there has been an increasing recognition of the cruciality of females' entrepreneurship in the economy. On top, the Egyptian government is implementing intensive programmes to boost entrepreneurship and revitalise micro, small and medium enterprises (MSMEs). According to the Central Agency for Public Mobilisation and Statistics, by 2030 Egypt aims to have womenfolk in 40% of their workforce (CAPMAS, 2021). Although the Egyptian constitution and the labour laws have been promoting females' access to the labour force, women's economic participation is low in Egypt (ILO, KILM statistics, 2016). Hence, women in Egypt need an encouraging environment to pursue their entrepreneurial activities; this should be through the removal of social, economic and educational barriers (Tiwari and Tiwari, 2007).

Toward the Future

With the recent advancement of ICTs and its growing contribution to the growth of economies, SM is spreading in scope and scale and is having a positive effect on the performance of various businesses and enterprises (Parveen et al., 2015). It is now providing a timely and effective strategic tool for small businesses (Parveen et al., 2016). It is specifically attractive for women as it addresses many of the challenges they have been facing; it supports them in identifying opportunities, having more access to markets and networks and engaging with customers (Gupta and Bose, 2019).

The literature indicates that the use of SM can be most beneficial to women entrepreneurs in low-income countries (Beninger et al., 2016). It provides self-generating and responsive platforms that can support women entrepreneurs in general (Ajjan et al., 2015) and in particular through useful tools that overcome the market access challenges faced by women when pursuing creating a new business (Beninger et al., 2016). The

SM penetration rate in Egypt has exceeded 47.4 % (i.e., 49 million users) (Kemp, 2021). Kemp (2021) confirmed that 79% of internet users in Egypt searched for a good/service to buy online, while 57% bought a product online and 40% used their mobile devices to purchase online. Egyptian users spend approximately three hours per day on SM, which is greater than the world's average. Egypt is one of the top 10 leading countries in terms of Facebook audience and active usage of Facebook per month. In addition, women are using SM extensively; they were recently 44% of Facebook users and 50.9% of Instagram users in Egypt (Kemp, 2020), thus they can easily make effective use of it, as well. These figures indicate the potential opportunities for businesses, given the vast online consumer base. This again signposts how operating businesses online is becoming recently vital in Egypt.

SM has been associated with women empowerment and agency primarily through two channels: its effect on expanding women's entrepreneurship and its positive impact on their personal lives stemming from them being part of a broader social network. Cesaroni et al. (2017) reviewing the very limited literature on SM and women entrepreneurs revealed that this new research area has few studies that focused on women entrepreneurs in emerging countries, including Egypt, where SM opens up new opportunities for female entrepreneurs and encourages the creation of new businesses run by women, given its connectivity power, flexibility and other attributes. Moreover, they showed that SM empowers women on various levels. On the personal level, it advances women's self-realisation. On the professional level, it helps women create online businesses with low investment and operating costs. On the family level, it significantly boosts women's negotiating power, and on the social level, it enables them to effectively participate in their social lives. This new trend of using SM to support entrepreneurial activities is called digital entrepreneurship, which can also be seen as the reconciliation of traditional entrepreneurship with the new way of creating and doing business in the digital era (Le Dinh et al., 2018).

Different scholars were able to link SM use and digital entrepreneurship to various outcomes of entrepreneurial activities. For example, it is argued that the use of SM by women entrepreneurs in the MENA region will increase their social capital and self-efficacy (Beninger et al., 2016). Beninger et al. (2016) conducted semi-structured interviews with 30 Egyptian women entrepreneurs, which exhibited that access to SM and social network support were important reasons for starting a business. Furthermore, the same research proposed that SM empowered women entrepreneurs through gaining financial autonomy and boosting their confidence, which led to becoming more independent.

There are other studies that show women entrepreneurial success based on SM use in several Arab countries; showed how Saudi Arabian women entrepreneurs used Instagram to start and operate their own online businesses; interviewed nine successful Emirati businesswomen and found that Instagram is heavily and effectively used by Emirati women entrepreneurs as a marketing tool for their home-based businesses, especially that it allows them to engage in business freely without any social pressures or discomforts.

There is also recent research that provided evidence that SM use has a positive effect on entrepreneurial performance in Egypt for both female and male entrepreneurs, in a study of more than 350 SMEs in the manufacturing sector (Fakhreldin et al., 2020). In depth, interviews were conducted in this study with two women entrepreneurs, one in the manufacturing and the other in the service sector. Both confirmed that SM had a positive impact on their business performance (Fakhreldin et al., in press). The owner and manager of a leather goods factory and shop (Exhibit 6.15) explained that SM replaced the need to open other branches for the shop she has in other areas in Cairo or other cities in Egypt. She uses Facebook and Instagram to receive the orders of what they want to choose from, and she sends the products to the customers at home with a representative. Furthermore, young female entrepreneurs in Upper Egypt (Exhibit 6.16) communicated how they can take advantage of opportunities because of the SM, which helped them access more markets and overcome rurality.

Another study that is based on data collected from 240 women entrepreneurs in the Greater Cairo area indicated that digital entrepreneurship resulted in higher levels of empowerment for women who are owners of micro-enterprises. Being engaged in digital entrepreneurship permits women to contribute to household income, which bolsters their negotiating and bargaining powers over household decisions (Cesaroni et al., 2017; Crittenden et al., 2019). This also has a positive impact on the health and educational outcomes of the household. As SM augments their social capital and participation within their communities, it reduces their isolation and improves their social lives (Melissa et al., 2013). Moreover, SM interaction boosts women's experience sharing, enhances their expressive abilities, and amplifies their feelings of being entitled to initiating change and confronting their tough conditions (Golzard, 2019). This is in line with the Theory of Social Psychology of Participation, which postulates that the

Exhibit 6.15 Owner-manager of a leather goods factory and shop;
photograph © the authors

increase in people's awareness with regard to their resources and rights happens by the virtue of participation within a group, which consequently empowers them to collectively initiate change.

Thus, the use of SM and engaging in digital entrepreneurship have a positive impact on the lives of women entrepreneurs who become empowered on a personal, relational — within their households and wider communities, and environmental levels (Crittenden et al., 2019). Women's empowerment characteristics can be in terms of positive changes in their

Exhibit 6.16 Young artisan woman from Upper Egypt; photograph © the authors

self-esteem; self-confidence; self-efficacy; opinions about: women's economic role, gender rights and power within the households; business confidence; autonomy; access to finance; saving and investing their business profits; contributing to household income; making household expenses, investment and other decisions; as well as having control over household assets.

Moving on now to consider available online resources, there is now easier access to resources through the internet and the use of SM, this opens opportunities for self-learning (Ajjan et al., 2015), for example, Google Maharat in Egypt, where they are training SMEs, start-ups and entrepreneurs on the importance of creating or moving their businesses online; they show them the basic tools and options using SM and making use of all the options and opportunities it provides. According to the results of another recent study, using SM led to an increase in sales volume, a positive impact on customer engagement (in terms of electronic word-of-mouth and customer inquiries) and brand performance (in terms of perceived brand image, customer loyalty and retention) of MSMEs in Egypt (Fakhreldin et al., in progress). SM also made it possible to decrease the cost of expansion and opening new branches of small women-owned enterprises in Egypt (Fakhreldin et al., in press). The product is delivered to the customers home, where they can also examine a variety and choose, then buy; thus, providing a similar service like the one that used to be provided in Cairo in the 1940s and 1950s, when the product and/or service arrived the door of the consumer (Dana, 2012).

Women worldwide are seeking new economic opportunities through enterprise creation. As highlighted by several scholars, female entrepreneurs play a vital role in economic growth and poverty reduction (Brush and Cooper, 2012). Nevertheless, as indicated previously, women entrepreneurs still face more challenges than their male counterparts when pursuing new venture creation in the Egyptian context. They experience discrimination and hardships in many areas, especially when it comes to accessing financial resources (Ojediran and Anderson, 2020), mobility, networks and business skills, all of which are needed to successfully run a business (Melissa et al., 2013). The gender gap report of 2020 showed that there are 11 MENA countries in the lowest 10% of the 153 countries listed/examined in the report. Egypt is number 134 out of 153; in the 'economic participation and opportunity' component Egypt is number 140 (Crotti et al., 2020). This demonstrates the challenging situation of women in Egypt and the region.

Nowadays, MSMEs are increasingly using SM, since it has been shown to enhance their overall competitiveness and visibility (Aboelmaged, 2018). SM has expanded and eased up the possibilities of business creation for Egyptian women. It has brought new hopes to women entrepreneurs by bringing flexible entrepreneurial opportunities that free women from the many limitations and challenges they face (Duncombe et al. 2005).

Digital technology can provide many benefits to entrepreneurs, such as faster communication unrestrained from time and space, effectively making access to networks and markets convenient (Hansen, 2019). In a broader perspective, digital entrepreneurship facilitates the exploration and exploitation of entrepreneurial opportunities because of leveraging digital technologies and digital business models (Soltanifar et al., 2021). This has led to the creation and expansion of digital economies (Soltanifar et al., 2021), which observes an increasing number of entrepreneurs participating in the sharing and exchange of knowledge and goods and services (Le Dinh et al., 2018). All the above is most relevant and important to women entrepreneurs, who usually have less access to resources compared to their male counterparts.

The impact of SM is different based on the context in a setting like Egypt. Female entrepreneurs need access to more basic technology — internet and basic infrastructure. Hence, policymakers aiming at boosting female entrepreneurship in Egypt need to target the informal economy, as well, and tailor digital interventions in harmony with the type of digital platforms available and predominant in the informal sector.

The potential benefits perceived from using SM are the driving force that led to its adoption; therefore, it is most important to educate and train Egyptian female entrepreneurs on the advantages of SM use for their enterprises. On the practical side, more attention should be given to providing advanced capacity building in the area of IT and SM use (including programmes and infrastructure) to support the entrepreneurs in the creation and development of their new/existing small ventures (Fakhreldin et al., 2020). The enhancement of the country's IT and SM infrastructure is to be considered a key priority, as it is a basic need for the continuous development and success of the MSMEs.

References

Aboelmaged, M. (2018), "The Drivers of Sustainable Manufacturing Practices in Egyptian SMEs and Their Impact on Competetive Capabilities: A PLS-SEM Model," *Journal of Cleaner Production* 175, pp. 207–221.

Adam, S., A. Mahrous, and W. Kortam (2017), "The Relationship Between Entrepreneurial Orientation, Marketing Innovation and Competitive Marketing Advantage of Female Entrepreneurs in Egypt," *International Journal of Technology Management and Sustainable Development* 16(2), pp. 157–174.

Ajjan, H., F. Fabian, D. Tomczyk, and H. Hattab (2015), "Social Media Use to Support Entrepreneurship in the Face of Disruption," *Journal of Developmental Entrepreneurship* 20(3), pp. 1–27.

Alkasmi, A., O. Hamamsy, L. Khoury, and A. Syed (2018), *Entrepreneurship in the Middle East and North Africa: How Investors can Support and Enable Growth,* Dubai: Digital McKinsey.

Beninger, S., H. Ajjan, R. Mostafa, and V. Crittenden (2016), "A Road to Empowerment: Social Media Use by Women Entrepreneurs in Egypt," *International Journal of Entrepreneurship and Small Business* 27, pp. 308–332.

Brush, C., and S. Cooper (2012), "Female Entrepreneurship and Economic Development: An International Perspective. *Entrepreneurship & Regional Development* 24, pp. 1–6.

CAPMAS (2020), *Statistical Yearbook,* Egypt: Central Agency for Public Mobilization and Statistics.

CAPMAS (2021), *Egypt in Figures,* Egypt: Central Agency for Public Mobilization and Statistics.

Cesaroni, F. M., P. Paoloni, and P. Demartini (2017), "Women in Business and Social Media: Implications for Female Entrepreneurship in Emerging Countries," *African Journal of Business Management* 11 (14), pp. 316–326.

Constant, L., I. Edochie, P. Glick, J. Martini, and C. Garber (2020), *Barriers to Employment that Women Face in Egypt: Policy Challenges and Considerations.* Sanata Monica, CA: RAND.

Cormack, R. (2021), *Midnight in Cairo: The Divas of Egypt's Roaring '20s,* London: Saqi Books.

Crittenden, V. L., W. F. Crittenden, and H. Ajjan (2019), "Empowering Women Micro-Entrepreneurs in Emerging Economies: The Role of Information Communications Technology," *Journal of Business Research* 98, pp. 191–203.

Crotti, R., T. Geiger, V. Ratcheva, and S. Zahidi (2020), *Global Gender Gap Report 2020,* Geneva, Switzerland: World Economic Forum, http://www3.weforum.org/docs/WEF_GGGR_2020.pdf

Dana, L.P. (1993), "Environments for Entrepreneurship: A Model for Public Policy and Economic Development," *The Journal of Entrepreneurship* 2(1), pp. 73–86.

Dana, L.P. (2000), "Economic Sectors in Egypt and Their Managerial Implications," *Journal of African Business* 1, pp. 65–81.

Dana, L.P. (2012), "Learning From Lagnado About Self-Employment & Entrepreneurship in Egypt," *International Journal of Entrepreneurship & Small Business* 17(1), pp. 140–153.

Danielson, V. (1991), "Artists and Entrepreneurs: Female Singers in Cairo During the 1920s," in N. A. Keddie, ed., *Women in Middle Eastern History: Shifting Boundaries in Sex and Gender.* New Haven, CT: Yale University Press, pp. 292–309.

Drucker, P. (1970), "Entrepreneurship in Business Enterprise," *Journal of Business Policy* 1, pp. 3–12.

Duncombe, R., R. Heeks, S. Morgan, and S. Arun (2005), *Supporting Women's ICT-Based Enterprises: A Handbook for Agencies in Development,* Manchester, United Kingdom: Institute for Development Policy and Management (IDPM).

Elam, A., C. Brush, P. Greene, B. Baumer, M. Dean, and R. Heavlow (2019), *GEM Women's Entrepreneurship Report,* London, United Kingdom: Global Entrepreneurship Research Association, London Business School.

ElAshmawy, K. (2016), *The Social and Economic Empowerment of Women in Egypt: Toward a New Development Paradigm, Policy Brief 036,* Giza, Egypt: Egypt Network for Integrated Development.

El Mahdi, A. (2020, March 13), *Women Entrepreneurs in Egypt (S. Gateway, Interviewer),* Giza, Egypt: Egypt Network for Integrated Development.

ELShorbagi, S., A. Rizk, and A. Kamal (2017), *Women's Entrepreneurship Development Assessment: Egypt,* Cairo, Egypt: ILO Decent Work Team for North Africa and Country Office for Egypt and Eritrea.

Fakhreldin, H., A. Ayman, and R. Miniesy (2020), Social Media Use and its Effect on the Performance of MSMEs. Proceedings of the European Conference on Innovation and Entrepreneurship, ECIE, Rome, pp. 251–260.

Fakhreldin, H., A. Ayman, and R. Miniesy (in press), "The Impact of Social Media Use on Firm Performance: A Study of Egyptian Micro, Small and Medium Enterprises (MSMEs)," *International Journal of Entrepreneurship and Small Business.*

Farrugia, M. (2002), *The Plight of Women in Egyptian Cinema (1940s - 1960s).* Unpublished doctoral dissertation, The University of Leeds, Leeds, https://etheses.whiterose.ac.uk/251/1/uk_bl_ethos_436769.pdf

Farzanegan, M. (2014), "Can Oil-Rich Countries Encourage Entrepreneurship," *Entrepreneurship & Regional Development* 26, pp. 706–725.

Fertat, PA. (2016, October 4), "Les pionnières oubliées du cinéma arabe Aziza Amir, la marraine du cinéma égyptien," https://www.libe.ma/Les-pionnieres-oubliees-du-cinema-arabe-Aziza-Amir-la-marraine-du-cinema-egyptien_a79180.html

GEM (2021), *2020/2021 Global Report,* London: Global Entrepreneurship Research Association, London Business School. https://www.gemconsortium.org/file/open?fileId=50691

Ghafar, A. A. (2016), *Educated But Unemployed: The Challenge Facing Egypt's Youth,* Doha: Brookings Doha Center.

Golzard, V. (2019), "Economic Empowerment of Iranian Women Through the Internet," *Gender in Management: An International Journal 35(1),* pp. 1–18. http://dx.doi.org/10.1108/GM-11-2017-0145

Gupta, G., and I. Bose (2019), "Strategic Learning for Digital Market Pioneering: Examining the Transformation of Wishberry's Crowdfunding Model," *Technological Forecasting and Social Change* 146, pp. 865–876.

Guttman, A. (2015, November 29), "10 Top Cities Around the World to Launch Your Startup," https://www.forbes.com/sites/amyguttman/2015/11/29/top-10-cities-in-the-world-to-launch-your-startup-some-may-surprise-you/?sh=3a5bc75e7e57

Hansen, B. (2019), "The Digital Revolution – Digital Entrepreneurship and Transformation in Beijing," *Small Enterprise Research* 26(1), pp. 36–54.

ILO (2011, April 5), "Youth Unemployment in the Arab World is a Major Cause for Rebellion," https://www.ilo.org/global/about-the-ilo/mission-and-objectives/features/WCMS_154078/lang--en/index.htm

ILO (2016), *Key Indicators of the Labour Market (KILM),* Geneva, Switzerland: International Labour Office.

IMF (2020, September 1), "Arab Republic of Egypt: Request for Purchase Under the Rapid Financing Instrument-Press Release; Staff Report; and Statement by the Executive Director for the Arab Republic of Egypt," https://www.imf.org/en/Publications/CR/Issues/2020/09/01/Arab-Republic-of-Egypt-Request-for-Purchase-Under-the-Rapid-Financing-Instrument-Press-49724

Ismail, A., A. Tolba, S. Barakat, H. Meshreki, and S. Ghalwash (2017), *GEM, Egypt National Report,* Cairo: Global Entrepreneurship Monitor.

Kemp, S. (2020, 17 February), "Digital 2020: Egypt," https://datareportal.com/reports/digital-2020-egypt?rq=egypt

Kemp, S. (2021, February 11), "Digital 2021: Egypt," https://datareportal
.com/reports/digital-2021-egypt?rq=egypt

Knight, F. H. (1921), *Risk, Uncertainty and Profit*, Boston and New York:
Houghton Mifflin.

Le Dinh, T., M. Vu, and A. Ayayi (2018), "Toward a Living Lab for
Promoting the Digital Entrepreneurship Process," *International
Journal of Entrepreneurship* 22(1), pp. 1–17.

Loveluck, L. (2012), *Education in Egypt: Key Challenges*, London, United
Kingdom: Chatham House.

Mahrous, A. (2019), "Female Entrepreneurship in Egypt: New Theoretical
and Public Policy Implications," *Marketing and Management of
Innovations* 1, pp. 151–160.

Melissa, E., A. Hamidati, M. S. Saraswati, and A. Flor (2013), "Investigating
the Potentials of Social Media to Support Women Entrepreneurship
in Indonesian Urban Area," *Proceedings of the Sixth International
Conference on Information and Communication Technologies and
Development* 13, pp. 92–95.

NCW (2017), *National Strategy for the Empowerment of Egyptian Women
2030*, Cairo: National Council for Women.

OECD (2018), *Women's Political Participation in Egypt*, MENA Region:
OECD.

Ojediran, F. O., and A. Anderson (2020), "Women's Entrepreneurship in
the Global South: Empowering and Emancipating?" *Administrative
Sciences* 10 (4), pp. 87–119.

Ojong, N., A. Simba, and L.-P. Dana (2021), "Female Entrepreneurship in
Africa: A Review, Trends, and Future Research Directions," *Journal
of Business Research* 132, pp. 233–248, https://doi.org/10.1016/j.
jbusres.2021.04.032

Parveen, F., N. Jaafar, and A. Sulaiman (2015), "Social Media Usage and
Organizational Performance: Reflections of Malaysian Social Media
Managers," *Telematics Informatics* 32, pp. 67–78.

Parveen, F., N. Jaafar, and S. Ainin (2016), "Social Media's Impact on
Organisational Performance and Entrepreneurial Orientation in
Organisations," *Management Decision* 54, pp. 2208–2234.

Soltanifar, M., M. Hughes, and L. Göcke (2021), *Digital Entrepreneurship:
Impact on Business and Society*, Cham: Springer.

Tiwari, S., and A. Tiwari (2007), *Women Entrepreneurship and Economic
Development*, New Delhi, India: Sarup & Sons.

UNIDO (2018), *Women's Empowerment Through Inclusive and Sustainable Industrial Development in the MENA Region*, Vienna, Austria: UNIDO.

Van Heel, K. D. (2015), *Mrs Tsenhor: A Female Entrepreneur in Ancient Egypt*, Cairo, Egypt: The American University in Cairo Press.

World Bank (2019), "Labor Force Participation Rate, Female," https://data.worldbank.org/indicator/SL.TLF.ACTI.FE.ZS?locations=EG

World Bank (2021), *Egypt's Economic Update — April 2021,* Washington, DC: World Bank Group.

© 2022 World Scientific Publishing Company
https://doi.org/10.1142/9789811236600_0007

Chapter 7

Women Entrepreneurs in Sudan

Ekaterina Vorobeva

The Research Centre for East European Studies
The University of Bremen, Klagenfurter Straße, 8, D-28359 Bremen, Germany

Abstract

Since improvements in a political course during the past years, female entrepreneurship in Sudan has been on the rise. Nevertheless, due to the prevalent culture of patriarchy and discriminatory laws undermining equality of genders, women still face numerous constrains to the generation of human, social and financial capital. While men are considered the main drivers of national economic development, women's potential to raise economic growth remains barely realised. To conclude, women are not accepted as equal economic actors in Sudan. Recent positive political changes place high hope for the enhancement of women's position in the economic life of the country.

Keywords: Sudan, Africa, women entrepreneurship, female entrepreneurship, minority entrepreneurship.

Introduction

During the past decades, Sudan has struggled to establish peace and economic prosperity on its territory. Civil conflicts (see Exhibit 7.1), environmental crisis, embargo imposed by Western states, exacerbating poverty, political instability and the loss of the biggest share of Sudan's oil production due to the separation of South Sudan in 2011 posed many challenges to the country on its way to well-being (Ismail et al., 2017; Khattab et al.,

Exhibit 7.1 Dinka tribe, South Sudan; photograph courtesy of unsplash.com

2017; Musa, 2014). Annual inflation reached 550% in 2016 and 370% in the following year (Khattab et al., 2017). Due to the above mentioned reasons, with the exception for agriculture, other sectors of Sudan's economy remain underdeveloped (Musa, 2014; Pitamber, 2001). Being generally relatively high, unemployment spreads unequally across the population harshly affecting the young and women.

Since 1990, aiming at boosting its hampered economic growth, the Sudanese government took the course on support and promotion of entrepreneurship among its citizens (Musa, 2014). Nevertheless, despite some improvements regarding starting and developing a private company (Arabi and Abdelgadir, 2020; Gangi and Timan, 2013), enterprises still face numerous obstacles in Sudan. Thus, success of the political course proved to be partial (Gangi and Timan, 2013; Musa, 2014). Survival rates among SMEs stay low (Khattab et al., 2017). Due to inability of the local government to address accumulated crucial issues in business law, within the last 5 years Sudan's position in the rating on ease of doing business was declining. According to the World Bank's Doing Business Report, in 2020, Sudan occupied 171 position (out of 190 world economies) while in 2016 it ranked 159 (World Bank, 2016; World Bank, 2020). In more detail, the poor performance of Sudan can be attributed to the refusal of the Sudanese government to accept amendments to the Companies Act. This political decision froze development in credit access, minority investors' protection and insolvency resolution (World Bank, 2020).

Constraints to entrepreneurship in Sudan can be roughly divided into two main groups: those related to activities of established enterprises, and ones concerning facilitation of entrepreneurship. The former includes limited access to funding, insufficient policies and support services, bureaucracy, inadequate infrastructure and difficulties with registration of property rights (Arabi and Abdelgadir, 2020; Musa, 2014). Even though the government recommended banks to allocate 12% of their portfolios for financial support of small and medium-sized businesses, the actual share of SMEs in banks' portfolios does not exceed 5% (Abubakar, 2015). The second group of constraints encompasses lack of relevant education and training, unavailability of mentors and incubators as well as cultural attitudes to business activities and risk-taking. For example, Gangi (2015) claims that higher education institutions failed to nurture entrepreneurial mentality among students.

The named obstacles disproportionately affect women; females remain disadvantaged and form a minority group on the entrepreneurship arena (Musa, 2014). Due to the culture of patriarchy and negative attitudes toward female (self-)employment, Sudanese women struggle to engage with entrepreneurship; they often suffer from limited access to the generation of human, financial and social capital (Elnur, 2015). Sudan still occupies one of the lowers positions in the United Nations Development Programme's (UNDP) International Human Development Indicators, namely, 170 out of 189 studied countries (UNDP, 2020). As the UNDP report for 2020 illustrates, together with more years of schooling, Sudanese males' gross national income per capita proved to be three times higher than the one of females demonstrating huge income inequality between the genders (UNDP, 2020). Summarising findings of previous studies, the present chapter aims at exploring the position of female entrepreneurship in Sudan's business market into more depth.

Historical Overview

Despite recent positive political changes and the ouster of the dictator Omar al-Bashir in 2019, Sudan remains affected by results of the former economic governance. Since the military coup of 1989 when the National Islamic Front (NIF) came to power, Islamisation of the economy slowed down the progress in banking system, freedoms of economic activities and access to resources (Musa, 2014). Nevertheless, in 1990, the government recognised a crucial role of private companies in the economic development of the state and introduced Sudan's Structural Programme (SAP). The Programme aimed at liberalisation of the economy through transfer of leadership in the state's economic development from the public enterprise sector to the private one (Musa, 2014). SAP's goal appeared to be more than ambitious, namely, to remove all existent legal and economic constraints to entrepreneurship and foreign investment. At the national level, significant improvements took place in infrastructure, property registration, liberalisation of prices and wages, and reduction of tax rates (Gangi and Timan, 2013). Later on, Sudan engaged into a dialogue with the IMF to get necessary assistance in implementation of macroeconomic reforms. Following the SAP, the Ten-Year Comprehensive Strategy (1993–2003) and the Five-Year Plan (2005–2010) continued emphasising the importance of the private sector for Sudan's economic development (Gangi and Timan, 2013). In 2005, Microfinance Policy was introduced in order to provide SMEs with necessary financial means; among its main aims was also to ensure that females have access to financial services (Elnur, 2015).

The Twenty-Five-Year National Strategy of 2007–2031 was one of the first initiatives bringing up the issue of employment, entrepreneurial activities and equal rights of women. The Strategy generally committed to enhancing justice and equality, nurturing leadership, reducing poverty, developing rural areas and supporting the private sector. In respect to women's rights, it acknowledged the need of skills enhancement, increase in their role as social and economic actors, and development of traditional female industries such as needlework and pottery (Musa, 2014). The Strategy even declared a war against traditions negatively affecting women's participation in the economic life (Musa, 2014). These policies have resulted in some positive trends; for instance, in 2012, one quarter in the Sudanese Parliament was represented by women, the share larger than in some Western economies (Musa, 2014). However, they also imposed some limitations on females' employment. For example, the Sudanese Labour Law specified that women are prohibited from health-threatening and hard physical work as well as from working at night, between 10 pm and 6 am (Tønnessen, 2019).

In line with the political course, many projects and organisations have emerged to assist women in acquiring relevant skills, accessing funding and engaging with entrepreneurship. Hawa Charitable Organisation, Businesswomen Department of the National Congress, the Sudanese Businesswomen Secretariat (SBS) and the Sudanese Businesswomen Development Centre (SBWDC) are a few cases in point. Moreover, various projects aimed at creation of general positive entrepreneurship environment for entrepreneurs of all genders. For instance, the Graduate Employment National Fund (GENF) received thousands of applications to enrol in training and funding programmes for would-be businessmen and businesswomen (Arabi and Abdelgadir, 2020). Sudan Startup Weekend, Mashrouy Programme, Entrepreneurship Development Centres, Sudanese Ryadah Centre, Sudanese Eibdah Centre and BADEER contributed to acquisition of relevant skills and finances among Sudanese entrepreneurs (Khattab et al., 2017).

Women and Entrepreneurship

Sudanese Female Entrepreneurs: Characteristics, Motivations and Effects

Although entrepreneurship in Sudan in general and female entrepreneurship in particular became a topic of research relatively recently, several studies have already explored main characteristics, obstacles and motivations of Sudanese businesswomen. Even though the precise statistic is often absent, the number of Sudanese female entrepreneurs is expected to be much lower than the one of males despite the recent increase (Mansour and Gangi, 2020; Musa, 2014). Said and Enslin (2020) claim that 8.2% of residents in the capital of the country Khartoum is represented by businesswomen. According to quantitative studies, majority of female entrepreneurs are in their 30s (Mansour and Gangi, 2020; Siddig and Hegazi, 2014). Higher education proved to pull women into entrepreneurial activities (Khattab et al., 2017; Mansour and Gangi, 2020; Siddig and Hegazi, 2014). Being married is positively correlated with female entrepreneurship in Sudan (Mansour and Gangi, 2020). Due to the labour market exclusion, lack of prior work experience is another distinctive feature of Sudanese businesswomen (Badawi et al., 2008; Mansour and Gangi, 2020). Majority of female enterprises appear to be micro-level with no employees (Welsh et al., 2013). Interestingly, women don't involve other family members in their activities: Welsh et al.'s (2013) research reports that 88% of studied female enterprises in Sudan did not employ any immediate family members. While men can enjoy loans from banks, self-financing proved to be the only widely available funding option for female entrepreneurs (Mansour and Gangi, 2020; Siddig and Hegazi, 2014). Finally, Khattab et al. (2017) found that serial entrepreneurship might be quite widespread in Sudan, although popularity of the phenomenon among women is unknown.

Being marginalised in the labour market and entrepreneurship environment, struggling to maintain families and adjust to social norms, women tend to engage into industries with low-entry barriers and flexible working hours, which also entails scarce profits, limited scale and low productivity (Badawi et al., 2008; Welsh et al., 2013). Majority of females' enterprises are located in the industries of food, services and retail trade (Khattab et al., 2017; Mansour and Gangi, 2020; Welsh, 2016). Due to the existent restrictions to women's movement and presence in the public space, many females involved in informal sectors often work from the safety of their *harem* (Steel, 2017). For example, women represent a powerful force in the informal agricultural sector of Sudan, where they account for 70% of the total workforce (Welsh, 2016). Women are seen shopping in markets, but vendors tend to be men (see Exhibit 7.2, 7.3 and 7.4).

Motivations to engage with entrepreneurship significantly differ among various groups of females, highlighting the importance of urban/rural background, class and marital status (Nada, 2010; Steel, 2017). Although push and pull motivations to start a business proved to be mixed rather than strictly separated (Vorobeva, 2020), in the case of Sudanese women the two main groups, necessity-driven and professional/personal realisation-driven, were identified by previous studies. Talking about the former, spreading poverty, civil conflicts, environmental factors as well as migration of males abroad made many women heads of their families and, in some cases, the only breadwinners (Badawi et al., 2008; Mansour and Gangi, 2020; Said and Enslin, 2020). Tønnessen (2019) maintains that only 28% of Sudanese women enjoy salaried work; thus, many women are pushed into self-employment as the only available option to support their families. Moreover, as the study of Welsh (2016) indicates, rural women might be more often necessity-driven than female residents of cities. For the second group of women, the desire for self-fulfilment and professional realisation as well as search for entertainment to diversify their housewives' routines might be reasons behind entrepreneurial activities (Mansour and Gangi, 2020; Steel, 2017).

Exhibit 7.2 Khartoum market; photograph by Ammar Hreib used with permission

Exhibit 7.3 Sudanese food table; photograph courtesy of Pixabay

Exhibit 7.4 Tea made from hibiscus is known as *karkadeh*; photograph © Léo-Paul Dana

The effects of entrepreneurial activities of Sudanese women on their families and society are numerous, both positive and more problematic. They lifted their families out of poverty, provided children with education and healthcare, satisfied own basic needs and reduced general unemployment (Musa, 2014; Steel, 2017). Through self-employment, women significantly improved their income: Welsh et al. (2013) claim that female entrepreneurs reported higher yearly incomes than the national average. While managing businesses, they gain necessary confidence, empowerment and leadership skills. As a result, Siddig and Hegazi (2014) point at renegotiation of gender roles and growing influence of women over decision-making within their families. Finally, they represent positive role models to their families and an entire society and help other females to start enterprises (Badawi et al., 2008). However, the necessity to juggle responsibilities of household keepers, present mothers, obedient wives and successful businesswomen increases stress, makes working hours of women longer and, therefore, their personal well-being is exacerbated (Badawi et al., 2008; Siddig and Hegazi, 2014). Badawi et al. (2008) also state that women are more inclined than men to engage with second or multiple jobs. This increased pressure makes females willing to quit entrepreneurial activities more often than males, as suggested by the study of Mansour and Gangi (2020). In addition, children may receive less attention from their mothers due to self-employment of the latter. Finally, Badawi et al. (2008) claim that sons of businesswomen may tend to refuse their roles of family breadwinners later in life.

Gender-Specific and Intersectional Constraints to Entrepreneurship

Female entrepreneurship and employment still remain an issue of hot social debates in Sudan. The Main body of scholarly works points at prevalent negative attitudes toward females' economic activities (Badawi et al., 2008; Mansour and Gangi, 2020; Said and Enslin, 2020; Siddig and Hegazi, 2014; Steel, 2017; Tønnessen, 2019), while only the work of Musa (2014) claims the contrary. Getting to the heart of the phenomenon, since 1983, the introduction of the Islamic 'Sharia' law constrained women in their access to employment (Said and Enslin, 2020). Indeed, religiosity and the culture of patriarchy proved to have a negative effect on females' labour market participation (Tønnessen, 2019). In Sudan as well as many other MENA countries, 'the male breadwinner–female caregiver model' in division of labour within families prevails (Tønnessen, 2019, p. 227). Sudan's interpretation of the Islamic law made a crucial contribution into shaping gender norms; as a result, women were restricted to the roles of wives, mothers and household keepers, which are considered as secondary and less valuable activities. Girls' socialisation aims at nurturing such qualities as obedience and submission, which affects women's life ambitions and aspirations (Badawi et al., 2008). Moreover, despite the Constitution pronouncing equality of genders, in practice, the Muslim Family Law of 1991 declared the superior position of men over women (Tønnessen, 2019). For example, women must get the approval of their husbands to engage in salaried work. Punishment for disobedience is very strict; a woman loses her right for a husband's material support as well as custody of her children (Tønnessen, 2019). (Interestingly, if the permission is granted, the wages earned can be spent on any of the woman's personal needs without any obligation to contribute to a family budget.) Therefore, women in Sudan are not accepted as equal economic actors; they are constrained in their access to economic opportunities available to men.

As men are considered to be the sole breadwinners of families as well as main drivers of national economic growth, they are often prioritised in access to various resources. Badawi et al. (2008) argue that women are restricted in their access to land, loans, property, income, information and education. Therefore, as noticed by Pitamber (2001), females are subjected to differentiated informality in the treatment of authorities that use non-transparency of local laws to prevent women from taking full advantage of the local opportunity structure. Exclusion from financial services proved to be the main constraint to self-employment of females by several studies (Badawi et al., 2008; Elnur, 2015; Eltahir, 2018; Mansour and Gangi, 2020; Musa, 2014). The majority of women have to rely on informal ways of financing their enterprises, such as the *safra* mechanism described by Nada (2010) in the case of street vendors of Khartoum, or risk their savings putting at danger their families' well-being (Siddig and Hegazi, 2014). Moreover, as pointed out by Steel (2017), and Said and Enslin (2020), due to housewives' responsibilities, restrictions in free movements without male guardians and lack of prior employment, networks formed by women are scarce and seldom accommodating to encourage entrepreneurial activities.

Sudanese women are limited in their choice of professions and industries for economic activities; some jobs are considered to be dangerous or simply not suitable for women, according to the prevalent social norms. Indeed, sexual harassment toward working women has been previously reported (Badawi et al., 2008); although, protection of women should not take place at the expense of their freedoms. Because of the norms, even though females form a majority of university students, their spread across disciplines is strongly affected by social expectations. Thus, females opt for agriculture and healthcare more often while engineering and mathematics remain unpopular among women (Elhag and Abdelmawla, 2020). Moreover, as females rarely occupy senior positions, their leadership and management skills are less developed, which may negatively affect their abilities and aspirations to start their own enterprises (Elhag and Abdelmawla, 2020; Elnur, 2015). In addition, females in rural areas may still experience difficulties in access to primary education (Pitamber, 2001).

Along with motivations, as it was noted previously, challenges proved to be not only gender but also context, class, ethnicity, race and religion specific, introducing new axes into the debates (Pitamber, 2001). Indeed, previous research highlighted that it is particularly the intersection of gender with other identity categories that forms business experiences of female entrepreneurs (Vorobeva, 2019). Intersectional positions of female entrepreneurs in Sudan were studied from the perspective of increased vulnerability. Steel (2017) noted that the presence of women in the streets without male guardians has a class dimension in Sudan; to maintain social status, husbands of middle and high classes should keep their wives away from dangers of the streets in safety of *harem*. On the contrary, women of lower social classes and divorcees have to go to the streets to earn a livelihood. For instance, Nada's (2010) study twists the categories of gender, class, migration history and marital status. It demonstrates how displaced divorced female street vendors in Khartoum were pushed into the streets of the city to provide for their children, which revealed their low social status and made them susceptible to condemnation, danger and mistreatment. Thus, they suffer from inequalities of both the culture of patriarchy and the capitalist system of Sudan, as Nada (2010) concludes.

Toward the Future

Two years have passed since the removal of al-Bashir from power, which cleared the road to crucial economic and social changes in Sudan. Nevertheless, the country still suffers consequences of the ex-dictator's legacy. Establishing peace on its territory and stabilising the state's economy fall under main priorities of the current Sudanese government. The COVID-19 pandemic also contributed to slowing down the economic recovery of the state. Even though various challenges are still in place, some improvements have already occurred. For instance, in December 2020, after 27 years, the United States removed Sudan from the list of state sponsors of terrorism, which opened up new ways for Sudan to reintegrate into the global community. Moreover, in 2021, Sudan signed The Abraham Accords Declaration, which has a crucial impact on normalisation of political relations and economic cooperation with Israel (Exhibit 7.5). The agreement seeks to strengthen peace in the Middle East, to protect human dignity and freedoms, and to create a world where everyone can enjoy

The Abraham Accords Declaration:

We, the undersigned, recognize the importance of maintaining and strengthening peace in the Middle East and around the world based on mutual understanding and coexistence, as well as respect for human dignity and freedom, including religious freedom.

We encourage efforts to promote interfaith and intercultural dialogue to advance a culture of peace among the three Abrahamic religions and all humanity.

We believe that the best way to address challenges is through cooperation and dialogue and that developing friendly relations among States advances the interests of lasting peace in the Middle East and around the world.

We seek tolerance and respect for every person in order to make this world a place where all can enjoy a life of dignity and hope, no matter their race, faith or ethnicity.

We support science, art, medicine, and commerce to inspire humankind, maximize human potential and bring nations closer together.

We seek to end radicalization and conflict to provide all children a better future.

We pursue a vision of peace, security, and prosperity in the Middle East and around the world.

In this spirit, we warmly welcome and are encouraged by the progress already made in establishing diplomatic relations between Israel and its neighbors in the region under the principles of the Abraham Accords. We are encouraged by the ongoing efforts to consolidate and expand such friendly relations based on shared interests and a shared commitment to a better future.

For the Republic of Sudan:

Witnessed by:

Exhibit 7.5 The Abraham accords declaration signed by the Republic of Sudan

equal rights, 'no matter their race, faith or ethnicity'. It also emphasises the necessity to support commerce and realise human potential. In line with the values of equality and peace highlighted in the Declaration, it places some hope for improvements in the position of women in Sudan.

With respect to entrepreneurship in general including female entrepreneurship, there are several steps for the current government to take in order to boost economic growth of the country with the assistance of the private sector. For the private sector per se, more coherent regulatory framework is necessary (Arabi and Abdelgadir, 2020). Eltahir (2018) proposes creation of an authority, which will be solely responsible for law, regulations, support mechanisms, funding and other SME-related issues. Better access to information of available funding, support and cooperation opportunities should be ensured (Eltahir, 2018). According to Musa (2014), the reduction of taxes might have a positive impact on number and success rates of enterprises. Moreover, there is a need for more support mechanisms to encourage and sustain private enterprises in Sudan (Arabi and Abdelgadir, 2020). Upgrades in the infrastructure may benefit manufacturing and other sectors (Arabi and Abdelgadir, 2020; Musa, 2014). Universities and colleges should introduce new educational modules to contribute to nurturing entrepreneurship-related skills and competences.

Regarding female entrepreneurship in particular, future policies should stay aware of differences in obstacles and motivations that exist between male and female entrepreneurs in Sudan (Mansour and Gangi, 2020). Legal rights of women for equal treatment in the labour and business markets should be better protected (Badawi et al., 2008). Limitations in access to loans and other financial services should be removed (Badawi et al., 2008; Elnur, 2015; Musa, 2014). Media celebration of positive role models of Sudanese businesswomen and their stories of success proved to play a crucial role in encouraging entrepreneurship among women and, thus, should be enhanced (Badawi et al., 2008). Human and social capital of women needs to be increased through relevant education, support programmes and networking events (Mansour and Gangi, 2020). Difficult to orchestrate but crucial to implement, elimination of the culture of patriarchy, renegotiation of gender roles and a change in women's position in the society are necessary at the national level. Finally, concerning future research, longitudinal studies as well as both qualitative and quantitative research should be carried out on female entrepreneurship in Sudan to better understand the phenomenon and its implications for Sudan's economy (Badawi et al., 2008; Welsh et al., 2013).

References

Abubakar, H. A. (2015), "Entrepreneurship Development and Financial Literacy in Africa", *World Journal of Entrepreneurship, Management and Sustainable Development* 11, pp. 281–294

Arabi, N. G. A., and M. A. A. Abdelgadir (2020), "The Role of Ecosystem for Entrepreneurship Development in Sudan," *World Journal of Entrepreneurship, Management and Sustainable Development,* 16(4), pp. 307–326.

Badawi, S. M. El Z. A., W. A. A. Rahman, A. H. El Jack, and G. Lorenz, (2008), *Women in Food and Beverages Business in Urban Markets of Khartoum State* (Working Paper, No. 88/2008), Berlin, Germany: Humboldt-Universität zu Berlin, Wirtschafts- und Sozialwissenschaften an der Landwirtschaftlich-Gärtnerischen Fakultät. http://hdl.handle.net/10419/96465

Elhag, M. M., and M. A. Abdelmawla (2020), "Gender-Based Assessment of Science, Technology and Innovations Ecosystem in Sudan," *African Journal of Rural Development* 5(1), pp. 97–113.

Elnur, M. A. M. (2015), Problems Facing Women to Get Benefit From Micro Finance Projects in Khartoum State, Sudan. Conference Report, The 2nd Minia International Conference "Agriculture and Irrigation in Nile Basin Countries," March, Minia, Egypt. https://www.academia.edu/19841799/PROBLEMS_FACING_WOMEN_TO_GET_BENEFIT_FROM_MICRO_FINANCE_PROJECTS_IN_KHARTOUM_STATE_SUDAN

Eltahir, O. A. B. (2018), "Factors Affecting the Performance & Business Success of Small & Medium Enterprises in Sudan (Case Study: Omburman)," *International Journal of Small Business and Entrepreneurship Research* 6(6), pp. 14–22.

Gangi, Y. A. (2015), "The Role of Entrepreneurship Education to Achieve MDGs in Sudan," *International Journal of Sudan Research* 5(1), pp. 39–55.

Gangi, Y. A., and E. Timan (2013), "An Empirical Investigation of Entrepreneurial Environment in Sudan," *World Journal of Entrepreneurship, Management and Sustainable Development* 9(2–3), pp. 168–177.

Ismail, A., T. Schøtt, A. Bazargon, D. Dudokh, H. A. Kubaisi, M. Hassen, I. de la Vega, N. Chabrak, A. Annan, M. Herrington, and P. Kew (2017), "Middle East and North Africa (GEM Report)," https://www.gemconsortium.org/report/gem-2017-middle-east-and-north-africa-report

Khattab, I., S. S. Ahmed, and A. M. Ahmed (2017), "Determinants of Business Entrepreneurship Success in Sudan," *Business and Management Research Journal* 7(7), pp. 66–75.

Mansour, I. H. F., and Y. A. Gangi (2020), "Women Entrepreneur Motivations, Challenges, and Growth Aspiration: A Gender Lens Analysis in Sudan," *ASRIC Journal on Social Sciences & Humanities* 1, pp. 9–19.

Musa, E. A. (2014), *Emerging Women Entrepreneurs in Sudan: Individual Characteristics, Obstacles and Empowerment,* Augsburg: Rainer Hampp Verlag.

Nada, M. A. (2010), *Divorced Women Who Engage in Micro-entrepreneurship in Sudan: Out of the Frying Pan and Into the Fire?* Master's Thesis, https://idl-bnc-idrc.dspacedirect.org/handle/10625/50980

Pitamber, S. (2001), *The Role of Entrepreneurship in Realizing Sustainable Human Development in Africa. The Case of the Sudan* (Discussion Paper No. 33). Sudan Economy Research Group. Bremen: The University of Bremen. http://www.iwim.uni-bremen.de/files/dateien/1540_serg33.pdf

Said, I., and C. Enslin (2020), "Lived Experiences of Females With Entrepreneurship in Sudan: Networking, Social Expectations, and Family Support," *SAGE Open.* DOI: 10.1177/2158244020963131

Siddig, K., and M. O. Hegazi (2014), "The Role of Microenterprises in Empowering Women in Urban Sudan," EcoMod2014 7147, EcoMod. https://ideas.repec.org/p/ekd/006356/7147.html

Steel, G. (2017), "Navigating (Im)Mobility: Female Entrepreneurship and Social Media in Khartoum," *Africa* 87(2), pp. 233–252.

Tønnessen, L. (2019), "Women at Work in Sudan: Marital Privilege or Constitutional Right?" *Social Politics* 26(2), pp. 223–244.

UNDP (2020), "Human Development Report 2020. The Next Frontier: Human Development and the Anthropocene," http://hdr.undp.org/sites/default/files/hdr2020.pdf

Vorobeva, E. (2019), "Intersectionality and Policy-Making: Structural Barriers to Entrepreneurship for Black African Females in Finland," *Politeja* 16(6(63)), pp. 139–151.

Vorobeva, E. (2020), "Revision of Pull and Push Factors to Migrant Entrepreneurship," *Siirtolaisuus/ Migration* 46, pp. 37–39.

Welsh, D. H. B. (2016), "Women-Owned Family Businesses in Africa: Entrepreneurs Changing the Face of Progress," in M. Acquaah, ed., *Family Businesses in Sub-Saharan Africa: Behavioral and Strategic Perspective,* New York: Palgrave Macmillan, pp. 155–174.

Welsh, D. H. B., E. Memili, E. Kaciak, and S. Ahmed (2013), "Sudanese Women Entrepreneurs," *Journal of Developmental Entrepreneurship* 18(2), p. 1350013. doi:10.1142/S1084946713500131

World Bank (2016), *Doing Business 2016: Measuring Regulatory Quality and Efficiency,* Washington, DC: World Bank.

World Bank (2020), *Doing Business 2020,* Washington, DC: World Bank.

© 2022 World Scientific Publishing Company
https://doi.org/10.1142/9789811236600_0008

Chapter 8

Toward the Future

Helene Balslev Clausen
Aalborg University, Denmark

Nada Khachlouf
ICD Business School Paris, France

North Africa is a diverse region with a rich history of cultural heterogeneity (Julius, 2018). Despite many differences across the region, the marginalisation of women (see Exhibit 8.1) has long been widespread in this part of the world, as men dominated the business realm from transportation (Exhibit 8.2) to trade (see Exhibit 8.3).

This chapter revisits some of the themes of this book, including the dependence and marginalisation of women in North Africa. It summarises trends across North Africa and looks forward with recommendations and suggestions for future research and policy implications about women entrepreneurs in the region.

Research Avenues

The topics covered in this book offer a historical overview of women and entrepreneurship in different parts of the North African region with businesswomen often being prevented from realising their economic potential because of gender inequality. Authors also emphasised the gendered nature of the entrepreneurial ecosystem in which women entrepreneurs of North Africa are at a disadvantage. At the same time, the book highlights a growing recognition of the role that women in business play in their countries' economies. Female entrepreneurship in the North African region has been increasing and becoming more visible over the last decade. Despite the apparent benefits of increased levels of women's entrepreneurship in the region, women business owners report that they face a series of constraints when it comes to setting up or expanding a business. The lack of data has been recognised to hinder both understanding and systematic analysis of the constraints that women face in the business world, calling for further research on this topic.

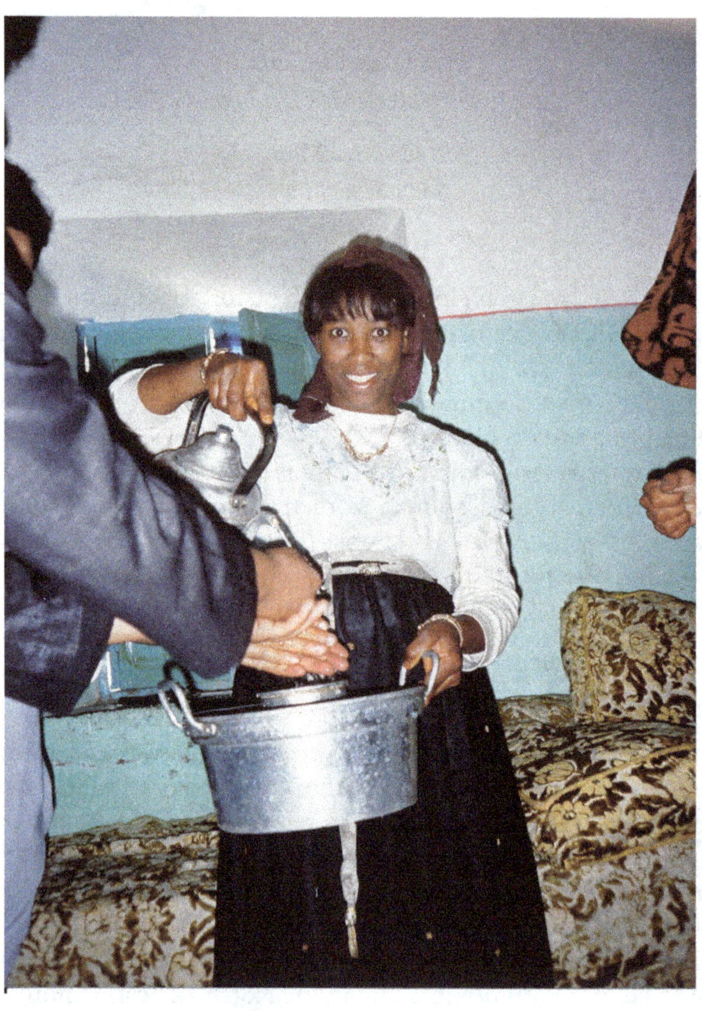

Exhibit 8.1 She was taught to aspire only to serve (Morocco); photograph © Léo-Paul Dana

Exhibit 8.2 Men in charge of deliveries; photograph © Léo-Paul Dana

Exhibit 8.3 Business in Sakakini (Egypt); photograph © Léo-Paul Dana

A core issue in North African female entrepreneurship research is to understand the critical role of the environment (political, economic, social, religious and cultural) in which women entrepreneurs are embedded. Different environment characteristics lead to diversified paths for women entrepreneurs to gain access to various resources (e.g., human, social, financial, and spiritual) that have been shown to be a critical component of entrepreneurial activity (Ojong et al., 2021; Rawhouser et al., 2017). Indeed, this book reflects an overemphasis on the resource constraints faced by female entrepreneurs in the North African context. Women entrepreneurs of North Africa still struggle with limited access to finance, technology and resources that hampers their capacity and efficiency to engage in entrepreneurial activities. In this perspective, more research is needed on how women entrepreneurs succeed in attracting the external resources they need to start their businesses. We call for further research that focuses on how female entrepreneurs, as a result of their embeddedness in hostile environments, develop innovative strategies to access and implement resources in a novel way.

As a relational resource, social capital (Putnam, 1995) plays a vital role in resource access. While social capital and networks have been conceptualised as relevant components in entrepreneurial ecosystems (Spigel, 2017), their role remains under-researched in female entrepreneurship. This calls future studies to focus on how female entrepreneurs successfully engage their social networks in different entrepreneurial phases. As pointed out by researchers comparing male and female entrepreneurs (e.g., Hattab, 2012; Sorenson et al., 2008), the feminine view is that the world is a network or web of relationships and that those relationships must be preserved. Accordingly, women often prefer to organise in networks and to create collaborative and cooperative relationships in order to obtain social and instrumental support. In this perspective, little is known on whether and how North African women entrepreneurs use their social capital to access resources that are specifically difficult for them to reach (e.g., financial resources). The interactions between the cultural context and the network orientation of female North African entrepreneurs could be of an important concern as cultural constraints affect the individual's response to opportunity (Dana, 1996). Future research could analyse how various cultural traits across different countries may generate differences in female entrepreneurs' social capital (network orientation) in North Africa and ultimately result in different resource/opportunity access strategies.

Another topical research avenue in female entrepreneurship in North Africa is to understand the role of changes such as the Arab spring that started in late 2010 in Tunisia and later impacted other parts of the North African region. Indeed, politically unstable contexts are likely to give rise to different types of female entrepreneurial ventures. Yet, after more than a decade, we know little about the nature of female-owned businesses in this particular context, including available resources and strategies to achieve success. It is noteworthy that, while leading to an unstable context, the Arab Spring movement is expected to help support female entrepreneurship, with the aspiration to secure more freedoms to disadvantaged societal classes.

Finally, it is important to mention that discussions and actions around gendered entrepreneurship research have most often followed simplistic stereotypes that focused narrowly on women's roles, assuming them to be either victims or 'sustainability saviours'. Extant research seems less sensitive to the significant role of religion, stereotypes and traditions in shaping the entrepreneurial activities (Dana, 2021; Dana et al., 2018). In this line of thought, the literature shows that different institutional settings (rules and regulations) are prone to deterministic types of gender-based discriminatory practices that constrain women entrepreneurship (Harrison et al., 2020). Of a critical issue in North Africa are the informal institutions, which are not widely researched within women entrepreneurship. The significance of informal practices, norms and regulations could provide valuable insights into inequitable ideologies, and cultural and religious practices. Further research is needed to show how gendered institutions, formal and informal (see Meis Mason et al., 2009) interact to explain female entrepreneurial activity in North Africa.

Policy Implications

Gender equality and women's empowerment stand high on the agenda of policymakers as well as on the current agenda of the Sustainable Development Goals. In order to address the marginalisation of women entrepreneurship in North Africa, national and regional governments' central concerns should be focused on how to create a space for women to voice their needs and aspirations reflecting their experiences and daily realities in highly patriarchal societies and to create participatory processes to help integrate women in knowledge regimes and decision-making processes. Participatory processes are likely to reduce potential structural and systemic hostile selection mechanisms that underpin the marginalisation of women entrepreneurship in North African countries (Montanari and Bergh, 2019). For example, in order to unleash the potential of women entrepreneurship, several promising policies and strategies have been put forward in the past decade to underpin and empower women (Cornwall, 2016) through training programmes that enhance their skills and strengthen their social capital as well as give them access to financial resources.

To sum up, future studies should focus on the contextual embeddedness of women's entrepreneurship of North Africa with a greater gender consciousness beyond biological sex categories. Indeed, the continued focus on male–female comparisons, with little or no attention to constructions of gender, reinforces subordination and thus restricts the development of female entrepreneurship research (Henry et al., 2016). Further conceptual research needs to be elaborated while overcoming the Western knowledge ontology in order to fine-tune the early involvement of gender to address the priorities for North African women and how they engage in participatory practices in the pursuit of their entrepreneurial interests. The Westernised conceptualisations of female entrepreneurship do not fairly and accurately take into account the socio-political, cultural and historical idiosyncrasies of the North African context (Dana et al., 2018). Theorising female entrepreneurship in North Africa would more accurately assess the role and position of (minority) women entrepreneurs in their entrepreneurial ecosystems helping the field to progress. At a practical level, addressing these issues would highlight the virtue of incorporating integration mechanisms in policies and practices aimed at fostering North African women entrepreneurs facing significant resource challenges.

References

Cornwall, A. (2016), "Women's Empowerment: What Works?" *Journal of International Development* 28, pp. 342–359, https://doi.org/10.1002/jid.3210

Dana, L. P. (1996), "Self-Employment in the Canadian Sub-Arctic: An Exploratory Study," *Canadian Journal of Administrative Sciences/ Revue canadienne des sciences de l'administration* 13(1), pp. 65–77.

Dana, L. P. (2021), "Religion as an Explanatory Variable for Entrepreneurship," in L. P. Dana, ed., *World Encyclopedia of Entrepreneurship*. Cheltenham, England: Edward Elgar.

Dana, L. P., V. Ratten, and B. Q. Honyenuga (2018), "Introduction to African entrepreneurship," in L. P. Dana, L. P., V. Ratten, and B. Q. Honyenuga, eds., *African Entrepreneurship*, Cham, Switzerland: Palgrave Macmillan, pp. 1–7.

Harrison, R. T., C. M. Leitch, and M. McAdam (2020), "Women's Entrepreneurship as Gendered Niche: The Implications for Regional Development," *Journal of Economic Geography* 20, pp. 1041–1067.

Hattab, H. (2012), "Towards Understanding Female Entrepreneurship in Middle Eastern and North African Countries. A Cross-Country Comparison of Female Entrepreneurship," *Education, Business and Society: Contemporary Middle Eastern Issues* 5(3), pp. 171–186.

Henry, C., L. Foss, and H. Ahl (2016), Gender and Entrepreneurship Research: A Review of Methodological Approaches," *International Small Business Journal* 34(3), pp. 217–241.

Julius, Lyn (2018), *Uprooted: How 3000 Years of Jewish Civilisation in the Arab World Vanished Overnight*, Portland, Oregon: Vallentine Mitchell.

Mason, A. M., L. P. Dana, and R. B. Anderson (2009), "A Study of Enterprise in Rankin Inlet, Nunavut: Where Subsistence Self-Employment Meets Formal Entrepreneurship," *International Journal of Entrepreneurship and Small Business* 7(1), pp. 1–23.

Montanari, B., and S. Bergh (2019), "A Gendered Analysis of the Income Generating Activities Under the Green Morocco Plan: Who Profits?" *Human Ecology* 47, p. 409417, https://doi.org/10.1007/s10745-019-00086-8

Ojong, N., A. Simba, and L. P. Dana (2021), "Female Entrepreneurship in Africa: A Review, Trends, and Future Research Directions," *Journal of Business Research* 132, pp. 233–248.

Putnam, R. (1995), "Bowling Alone: America's Declining Social Capital," *Journal of Democracy* 6(1), pp. 65–78.

Rawhouser, H., J. Villanueva, and S. L. Newbert (2017), "Strategies and Tools for Entrepreneurial Resource Access: A Cross-Disciplinary Review and Typology," *International Journal of Management Reviews* 19(4), pp. 473–491.

Sorenson, R. L., C. A. Folker, and K. H. Brigham (2008), "The Collaborative Network Orientation: Achieving Business Success Through Collaborative Relationships," *Entrepreneurship Theory and Practice* 32(4), pp. 615–634.

Spigel, B. (2017), "The Relational Organization of Entrepreneurial Ecosystems," *Entrepreneurship Theory and Practice* 41(1), pp. 49–72.

© 2022 World Scientific Publishing Company
https://doi.org/10.1142/9789811236600_bmatter

Contributors

Lyn S. AMINE is a Professor Emerita of Marketing and International Business at Saint Louis University (the United States), Distinguished Fellow of the Academy of Marketing Science, Senior Fulbright Scholar (Bahrain, Morocco), Past President of Women in the Academy of International Business and has taught at ISCAE and Al-Akhawayn University (Morocco) and Sultan Qaboos University (Oman).

Elhem BEN FATMA is associated with both the Faculty of Economics and Management, University of Sfax, in Tunisia, and the College of Business and Economics at Qassim University in Saudi Arabia.

Ezzeddine BEN MOHAMED is associated with both the Faculty of Economics and Management, University of Sfax, Tunisia, and the College of Business and Economics at Qassim University in Saudi Arabia.

Helene Balslev CLAUSEN is an Associate Professor of Global Tourism Development and Coordinator of Tourism Study Programme, at Aalborg University, in Denmark. She is an anthropologist with a background in migration studies and a keen interest in sustainable development, entrepreneurship, participation and innovation specialised in Latin America. Her contributions draw from a range of disciplines and in particular art-based methods across humanities and social- and political sciences. She has worked in Mexico, Chile, Colombia and Costa Rica, Morocco among others. She has been co-leader in major research projects funded by the Mexican Research Council (CONACYT) and Costa Rica's Research Council and is a board member in several Latin American–based development and sustainability networks. She has published extensively in Spanish as well as in English in journal articles, book chapters and edited several books. One of her recent articles about entrepreneurship, "Los norteamericanos que reinventaron a los pueblos de México. Los emprendedores extranjeros en la redefinición de la cultura y el turismo" (2020) in *Latin*

American Research Review was nominated at the Latin American Studies Association for its groundbreaking research. Her overall framework moves toward placing greater emphasis on excavating the diverse, creative, and pluri-verse world-view as a way forward for sustainability transitions.

A. Allan DEGEN is an Emeritus Professor at Ben-Gurion University of the Negev, Beer Sheva, Israel. After receiving his Ph.D. at Tel Aviv University, he joined Ben-Gurion University (1980), where he was Head of the Desert Animal Adaptations and Husbandry Unit (1985–2015) and Chairman of the Wyler Department of Dryland Agriculture (2001–2004 and 2013–2015). He was the incumbent of the Bennie Slome Chair for Desert Livestock Production (2004–2015) and served as the co-Editor-in-Chief of the *Israel Journal of Zoology* (1999–2007). Allan has studied the livelihood of ethnic groups in different countries and, in Israel, is doing research on Negev Bedouin. He has authored or co-authored 24 books or chapters and over 250 publications in peer-reviewed journals.

Hadia FAKHR EL DIN is a Professor of International Business in the Faculty of Business Administration, Economics and Political Science at the British University in Egypt. She is the Vice Dean of Teaching and Learning of the Faculty. She teaches International Business, International Management, Organisational Behaviour, modules related to Middle Eastern and International Economics. Her research interests include but not limited to the following areas: Organisational Theory and Development, International Business, International Management, Knowledge Management, International Entrepreneurship, Sustainable Development and SME Development.

Boufeldja GHIAT obtained his first degree in Industrial Psychology from Oran University (Algeria) in 1977, and his M.Sc. in 'Work Design and Ergonomics' from Birmingham University (UK) in 1981. He joined Nottingham University (UK) from where he obtained his Ph.D. in 1987. His thesis was about Assessing Organisational Effectiveness in Algeria. He is a Professor of Organisational Psychology at Oran 2, Mohamed Ben Ahmed University, Algeria. He held several positions at the university, most notably as a Head of the Department of Psychology, Head of the Scientific Committee of the Department of Psychology, Head of the Scientific Council of the Faculty of Social Sciences.

Robert D. HISRICH is the Bridgestone Professor of International Marketing and Entrepreneurship and Director of the Global Management Centre at Kent State University (2015 to present). He previously held the Garvin Chair of Entrepreneurship and Director of the Walker Centre of Global Entrepreneurship at Thunderbird Graduate School of Management (2005–2015). He has received Honorary Degrees from Chuvash State University (Russia) and from Miskolc University (Hungary) as well as two Fulbright Fellowships. Author of 46 books, one of which, Entrepreneurship, is in 14 languages and over 350 articles. Dr. Hisrich is on the faculty of universities around the world.

Nada KHACHLOUF is an Associate Professor in Entrepreneurship and Strategy at ICD Business School of Paris, and co-head of the Social Entrepreneurship pole. She holds a Visiting Professor position at JAMK School of Business (Finland). Her research interests revolve around entrepreneurship, family firms, knowledge networks and collaborative relationships. She is currently conducting research on family firm innovation strategies and devotes part of her research to the topical issue of entrepreneurial entry by disadvantaged minorities.

Lassaad MAKHLOUF is at the Faculty of Economics and Management University of Sfax Tunisia and associated with the Research Unit CODECI at the University of Sfax.

Rania MINIESY is an Associate Professor of Economics and the Acting Head of the Economics Department at the British University in Egypt. She is also the cofounder of the Experimental and Behavioural Economics Laboratory (EBEL). Rania was awarded her Ph.D. in Political Economy and Public Policy from University of Southern California. Her research interests are in the areas of growth and development, especially as related to MSMEs, gender and behavioural issues. She has published in numerous international academic journals and is the editor of the Scopus-indexed *Journal of Chinese Economic and Foreign Trade Studies*.

Amina OMRANE has earned her PhD in Management Science from the University of Jean Moulin (Lyon III) and IHEC-Carthage. She is currently an Associate Professor (HDR), authorised to supervise researches in management science and entrepreneurship at the University of Sfax, in Tunisia. Her research interests include but are not limited to Entrepreneurship, Strategic Management, Innovation, Sustainable Development, and SME

Business Development. She published numerous articles in peer-reviewed reputed journals (i.e., *IJESB, TCR, RIPME, IJBG, JAB, IJBE, FIIB Business Review, IJMP*) and international conference proceedings, as a researcher affiliated with ECSTRA research centre, IHEC-Carthage. Author of several books, Dr. Amina Omrane is currently editing other books revolving around sustainability issues, entrepreneurship, management, as well as SMEs' innovation and knowledge development perspectives.

Mirjana RADOVIĆ-MARKOVIĆ is a Professor of Entrepreneurship. She gained complete expert education from the Faculty of Economics, Belgrade University. She was elected to the position of full professor and principal research fellow in a number of universities world-wide. By invitation, she has given a number of lectures abroad. She has written 30 books and more than 250 peer journal articles. Professor Radović-Marković was awarded the first prize for the best science paper for 2017, Emerald Literati Awards, which is selected and awarded by Emerald July 2018.

Aidin SALAMZADEH is an Assistant Professor at the University of Tehran. His interests are start-ups, new venture creation and entrepreneurship. Aidin serves as an associate editor for *Revista de Gestão* and *Innovation & Management Review* (Emerald), as well as an editorial advisory *in The Bottom Line* (Emerald). Besides, he is the cofounder of the Innovation and Entrepreneurship Research Lab (UK) and a reviewer in numerous distinguished international journals. Aidin is a member of the European SPES Forum, the Asian Academy of Management, the Institute of Economic Sciences and Ondokuz Mayis University.

Christine SAMY is a Lecturer at Leeds Trinity University. She is currently pursuing a Ph.D. in Entrepreneurship at the University of Strathclyde. She is involved in multi-disciplinary and collaborative projects, bridging entrepreneurship with other disciplines such as cultural heritage, urban studies and anthropology. Christine's main research interests include female entrepreneurship, contextualised entrepreneurship, social entrepreneurship, and migrant and minority entrepreneurship. She is particularly interested in qualitative and creative research methods as well as contextual approaches for understanding entrepreneurial experiences.

Ekaterina VOROBEVA is an affiliated Ph.D. fellow at the Bremen International Graduate School of Social Sciences and an EU-researcher at the Research Centre for East European Studies, the University of Bremen. She previously worked in several research projects on forced migration, international migration and migrant entrepreneurship in Finland and Malta. Ekaterina co-authored scientific articles and book chapters published by SAGE Business Cases, *GeoJournal*, Palgrave Macmillan, the University of Turku and the University of Dhaka.

CPSIA information can be obtained
at www.ICGtesting.com
Printed in the USA
BVHW061423210622
640031BV00002B/46